CONTENTS

Introduction

1. Looking for a Home 13

Choosing your property 14
Purchasing a flat 14
Valuing a property 14
Leasehold Reform Act 1993 15
Viewing properties 15
Buying an old house 16
Renovation grants 17
Disabled facilities grant 17
Equalities Act 2010 17
Planning permission 17
Buying a listed building 18
Building in conservation areas 18
Buying a new home 18
Building guarantees 19
Websites 19
Buying a rented house 20
Right to buy 20
Shared Ownership 20
Self-build property 21
Key points 23

2. The Role of Estate Agents 25

Estate agents 25
Choosing an agent 26
Selling through more than one agent 26
Buying property using the internet 27
Selling property using the internet 27
Key points 28

3

3. Buying a property-The Practicalities 29

Budget   29
Deposit   29
Stamp duty   30
Other costs   30
Land registry   31
Energy Performance Certificates   31
Structural surveys   31
Mortgage fees   32
Buildings Insurance   33
Removals   33
Costs of moving   34
The process of buying a property   34
Making an offer   35
Putting your own home on the market   35
Exchange of contracts   36
Buying with a friend   36
Completing a purchase   36
Buying a property in an auction   36
Preparing for auction   37
Buying before auction   37
At the auction   37
Sale by tender   38
House swapping   38
Key points   40

4. More about mortgages 41

Lenders   41
Centralised lenders   41
Brokers and 'independent' advisors   42
How much can you borrow?   42

Mortgage market Review   43
Deposits   42
Help to Buy Scheme   44
Joint Mortgages   46
Main types of mortgages   46
What to do if given the wrong advice   48
How to complain   49
Borrowing and the internet   50
Key points   52

5. Selling your home   **53**

Estate Agents   53
DIY selling   53
Setting the price   53
Selling by auction   54
Key points   59

6. Conveyancing a Property   **60**

Legal ownership of property   60
Freehold property   60
Leasehold property   61
The lease   61
Check-points in a lease   63
Two systems of conveyancing   64
Registered and unregistered land   64
The key steps in conveyancing   65
Making enquiries before contract   66
Local land charges search   67
Local authority searches   68
Other searches   69
Other enquiries   70
The contract for sale   70

Procedures in the formation of a contract   71
The contents of a contract   71
Misdescription   72
Misrepresentation   73
Non-disclosure   73
Signing the contract   73
Exchanging contracts   74
Completion   74
Return of pre-contract deposits   75
The position of parties after exchange   75
Bankruptcy of the vendor   75
Bankruptcy of the purchaser   76
Death of vendor or purchaser   76
Key points   77

7. Planning Moving Arrangements   78

DIY moves   78
Using professionals   78
Websites   79
Contacting utilities   79

8. Buying and Selling in Scotland   81

Looking for property   81
Ownership of property in Scotland   81
House prices   82
The buying process   82
Surveys   82
Making an offer   82
Exchange of missives   82
Missives concluded   83
Searches   83
Selling a house or flat   83

The legal services of a solicitor   85
Accepting offers   85
Setting an entry date   86
Completion   87
Key points   88

9. Buying Overseas   89

General advice   89
Useful websites   90

10. Renting Out Your Property-Finding a Tenant   91

Letting Agents   91
Advertisements   93
The public sector   93
Company lets   93
Short-lets   95
Student lets   95
The DSS and housing benefit   96
Holiday lets   96
Showing the property to the tenant   97
Deposits   99
Rental guarantees   100
Key points   101

11. Items Provided Under a Tenancy   102

Furniture   102
Services   102
Insurance   103
Key points   105

12. The Type of Tenancy to Use   106

The assured tenant   108
The Assured Shorthold tenancy   108
Tenancy running on after fixed term   109
Evicting assured shorthold tenants   109
Security of tenure: The ways in which a tenant can lose
their home as an assured (shorthold) tenant   109
The mandatory grounds for possession   110
The discretionary grounds for possession of a property 111
Fast track possession   112
Raising rent-How frequently can a landlord raise the rent? 112
Key points   114

13. Joint Tenancies   115

Joint tenancies: the position of two or more people
who have a tenancy agreement for one property   115
Key points   117

14. Carrying Out Repairs and Improvements   118

Repairs and improvements generally: Landlord and tenants
obligations   118
Example of repairs a landlord is responsible for: 118
Reporting repairs to landlords   119
The tenants rights whilst repairs are being carried out 120
Can the landlord put the rent up after doing repairs? 120
Tenants rights to make improvements to a property   120
Disabled tenants   121
Shared housing. The position of tenants in shared houses
(Houses in Multiple Occupation)   121
Duty to take safety measures   121
The availability of grants   125

Sanitation health and hygiene   126
key points   127

15. Regaining Possession of a Property   **128**

Fast track possession   128
Going to court to end the tenancy   129
Key points   132

16. At the End of a Tenancy   **133**

When does the tenancy end?   133
Handover procedure   133
Tenants property left behind   134
Death of a tenant   135

17. Managing the Finances-Tax and Other Issues   **136**

Allowable expenses   136
Non-allowable expenses   137
Furnished residential lettings   137
Furnished holiday lettings   138
All letting properties   138
How much capital allowance can you claim?   138
Which year do expenses apply to?   139
Losses   139
Working out tax payable   139
Reporting profits to HMRC   139
Capital gains tax   140
Tax on furnished holiday lettings   143
Key points   143

19. Private Tenancies in Scotland   **144**

   Different types of tenancy   144
   Protected tenancies   144
   Grounds for possession   145
   Fair rent system   145
   Statutory tenancies   146
   Assured tenants   146
   Short-assured tenancies   147
   Recovery of possession   147
   Key points   149

Useful Addresses/a summary of useful websites

Index

****

INTRODUCTION

As time goes by, we either find ourselves in the middle of a housing market 'boom' or a 'bust'. Currently, at the time of writing, we are experiencing a rise in property prices, after a long recession. However, notwithstanding market conditions, the process of buying and selling a home remains probably the single most important activity undertaken by individuals in their lifetime. The money and effort involved means that it is a process that must be carried out effectively and with a clear knowledge of the elements involved.

When buying or selling a home, particularly buying, you will liase with a whole number of people, professional or otherwise: solicitors, estate agents, finance brokers, surveyors, banks and building societies and so on. All of these people play a vital role in the house purchase/sale transaction. All of these parties involved will have many years experience of property and not all of them will be acting in your own best interests.

Very often, the person who owns the property or who wishes to purchase a property is the one with the least knowledge of the process and is the one who stands to lose the most. When initially looking for a property, wrong decisions are made. The price paid for a property is quite often too high, with disastrous consequences later on. The condition of the property may leave a lot to be desired. There are many stories of people losing out on this single most important transaction. Unfortunately, it is a fact that if mistakes are made at the outset then you might spend the rest of your life recovering from the consequences.

This book also covers the key points of renting out a property and is meant to be of help to those who have decided to rent out their property for one reason or another. Like all areas of life, knowledge is a precious asset and can help you make informed decisions. This book will go some way to assist you in being able to make informed decisions and to understand more about the process of buying, selling and renting out a property.

1

Buying a Home-Looking for a Home

Obviously, where you choose to buy your house will be your own decision. However, it may be your first time and you may be at a loss as to where to buy, i.e. rural areas or urban areas, the type and cost of property or whether a house or flat. There are several considerations here:

Area

Buying in a built up area has its advantages and disadvantages. There are normally more close communities, because of the sheer density. However, it is true to say that some built up areas have become fragmented by population movement, "Yuppification" etc. Local services are closer to hand and there is a greater variety of housing for sale. Transport links are also usually quite good and there are normally plenty of shops.

Disadvantages are less space, less privacy, more local activity, noise and pollution, less street parking, more expensive insurance and different schooling to rural environments. The incidence of crime and vandalism and levels of overall stress are higher in built up, more urban areas. This is not the case with all built up areas. It is up to the buyer to carry out research before making a commitment. If you are considering buying in a rural area, you might want to consider the following: there is more detached housing with land, more space and privacy. However, this can be undermined by the "village" syndrome where everyone knows your business, or wants to know your business. There is also cleaner air and insurance premiums can be lower. Disadvantages can be isolation, loneliness, lower level of services generally, and a limited choice of local education.

Choosing your property

You should think carefully when considering purchasing a larger property. You may encounter higher costs, which may include:

- Larger, more expensive, carpeting
- More furniture. It is highly unlikely that your existing furniture will suit a new larger home.
- Larger gardens to tend. Although this may have been one of the attractions, large gardens are time consuming, expensive and hard work.
- Bigger bills
- More decorating
- Higher overall maintenance costs

Valuing a property

In the main, buyers will leave it to estate agents to offer a fair price, or market price for the house. In a period of spiralling house price inflation which is now thankfully over, although there was a re-occurrence of this in London, values were seemingly plucked out of the air. If you want to compare estate agents valuations with others then you can access one of the websites, such as www.hometrack or rightmove in order to gain a comparative value. Other sites are the Halifax, Nationwide, the Royal Institute of Chartered Surveyors, the National Association of Estate Agents and the Land Registry. You can also gain an idea of the valuation by looking in estate agents windows and assessing similar properties.

Purchasing a flat

There are some important points to remember when purchasing a flat. These are common points that are overlooked. If you purchase a flat in a block, the costs of maintenance of the flat will be your own. However, the costs of maintaining the common parts will be down to the landlord (usually) paid for by you through a service charge. There has been an awful lot of trouble with service charges, trouble between landlord and leaseholder. It has to be said that many landlords see service charges as a way of making profit over and above other income, such as ground rent, which is usually negligible after sale of a lease.

Many landlords will own the companies that carry out the work and retain the profit made by these companies. They will charge leaseholders excessively for works which are often not needed. The 1996 Housing Act (as amended by the Commonhold and Leasehold Reform Act 2002) attempts to strengthen the hand of leaseholders against unscrupulous landlords by making it very difficult indeed for landlords to take legal action for forfeiture (repossession) of a lease without first giving the leaseholder a chance to challenge the service charges.

Be very careful if you are considering buying a flat in a block – you should establish levels of service charges and look at accounts. Try to elicit information from other leaseholders. It could be that there is a leaseholders organisation, formed to manage their own service charges. This will give you direct control over contracts such as gardening, cleaning, maintenance contacts and cyclical decoration contracts. Better value for money is obtained in this way. In this case, at least you know that the levels will be fair, as no one leaseholder stands to profit.

Leasehold Reform Act 1993 as amended by the Commonhold and Leasehold Reform Act 2002
Under this Act, all leaseholders have the right to extend the length of their lease by a term of 90 years. For example, if your lease has 80 years left to run you can extend it to 170 Years. There is a procedure in the above Act for valuation. Leaseholders can also collectively purchase the freehold of the block. There is a procedure for doing this in the Act although it is often time consuming and can be expensive. There are advantages however, particularly when leaseholders are not satisfied with management.

Viewing properties
Before you start house hunting, draw up a list of characteristics you will need from your new home, such as the number of bedrooms, size of

kitchen, garage, study and garden. Take the estate agents details with you when viewing. Also, take a tape measure with you. Assess the location of the property. Look at all the aspects and the surroundings. Give some thought as to the impact this will have in your future life. Assess the building, check the facing aspect of the property, i.e., north, south etc. and check the exterior carefully. Earlier, I talked about the need to be very careful when assessing a property. When you have made your mind up, a survey is essential.

Look for a damp proof course - normally about 15cm from the ground. Look for damp inside and out. Items like leaking rainwater pipes should be noted, as they can be a cause of damp. Look carefully at the windows. Are they rotten? Do they need replacing and so on. Look for any cracks. These should most certainly be investigated. A crack can be symptomatic of something worse or it can merely be surface. If you are not in a position to make this judgement then others should make it for you.

Heating is important. If the house or flat has central heating you will need to know when it was last tested. Gas central heating should be tested at least once a year.

All in all you need to remember that you cannot see everything in a house, particularly on the first visit. A great deal may be being concealed from you. In addition, your own knowledge of property may be slim. A second opinion is a must.

Buying an old house

If you are considering purchasing an older house and making improvements then there are a number of things to think about: consider whether your proposed alterations will be in keeping with the age and style of the house, and neighbouring houses, particularly in a terrace. A classic mistake is that of replacing doors and windows with unsympathetic modern products. Again, salesmen will sell you anything and quite often won't provide the correct advice. If appropriate, you should consider contacting the Victorian Society or the Georgian Group for advice on preserving your home. Both offer leaflets to help you carry out appropriate restoration. It is often a good idea to employ an architect or surveyor to oversee any alterations you are considering. For local contractors contact the Royal Institute of British Architects or Royal Institute of Chartered Surveyors.

Renovation grants

These may be available from local authorities, although there are stringent requirements. They are means tested and the higher your income the more you are expected to pay. For further details you should contact your local authority direct.

Disabled facilities grant

A grant may be available to adapt a property for a disabled person, for example improving access into and around the home and adapting existing facilities within it. These grants are mandatory, but a discretionary grant is available to make a property suitable for the accommodation, welfare or employment of a disabled person. A leaflet, generally entitled Help for Disabled People with Adaptation and Other works, which can be obtained from your local authority, provides basic information.

Equalities Act 2010

The Equality Act 2010, with effect from October 2010, has introduced an obligation on all landlords to ensure that, if a disabled person requests it, suitable disabled access to common parts, and within common parts is available. Again, information is available from the local authority.

Planning permission

If you are considering alterations of a significant nature, either internal or external, you may need planning permission from your local authority. You may need planning permission if you plan to change the look or external aspect of the building or if you are intending to change the use.

You are allowed to carry out some work without planning permission, so it is worth contacting the local authority. You should also ask about building regulations. These are concerned with the materials and methods of building adopted. Regulations for work carried out in conservation areas are strict. The building control department at your local authority will be able to advise you about building regulations.

Buying a listed building

Buildings of architectural or historical interest are listed by the Secretary of State for National Heritage following consultation with English Heritage, to protect them against inappropriate alteration. In Wales, buildings are listed by the Secretary of State for Wales in consultation with CADW (Heritage Wales). In Scotland, they are listed by the Secretary of State for Scotland, in consultation with Historic Scotland. If you intend to carry out work to a listed building, you are likely to need listed building consent for any internal or external work, in addition to planning permission. The conservation officer in the local planning department can provide further information.

Buildings in conservation areas

Local authorities can designate areas of special architectural or historical significance. Conservation areas are protected to ensure that their character or interest is retained. Whole towns or villages may be conservation areas or simply one particular street. Strict regulations are laid down for conservation areas. Protection includes all buildings and all types of trees that are larger than 7cm across at 1.5m above the ground. There may be limitations for putting up signs, outbuilding or items such as satellite dishes. Any developments in the area usually have to meet strict criteria, such as the use of traditional or local materials.

This also applies to property in national parks, designated Areas of Outstanding Natural Beauty and the Norfolk or Suffolk Broads.

Whether or not a property is listed or is deemed to be in a conservation area will show up when your conveyancer carries out the local authority search.

Buying a new house

There are a number of benefits to buying a new house. You have the advantages of being the first occupants. There should not be a demand for too much maintenance or DIY jobs, as the building is new. There will, however, be a defects period which usually runs for 6 months for building and 12 months for electrical mechanical. During this period you should expect minor problems, such as cracking of walls, plumbing etc, which will be the responsibility of the builder.

Energy loss will be minimal. A new house today uses 50 per cent less energy than a house built 15 years ago; consider the savings over an older property. An energy rating indicates how energy efficient a house is. The National House Building Council uses a rating scheme based on the National Energy Services Scheme, in which houses are giving a rating between 0 and 10. A house rated 10 will be very energy efficient and have very low running costs for its size. Security and safety are built in to new houses, smoke alarms are standard and security locks on doors and windows are usually included.

When the house market is slow developers usually offer incentives to buyers, such as cashback, payment of deposit etc. Sometimes they offer a part exchange scheme. These are definitely worth looking into. However, with part exchange you may not get the price you were looking for.

Building Guarantees
All new houses should be built to certain standards and qualify for one of the building industry guarantees. These building guarantees are normally essential for you to obtain a mortgage and they also make the property attractive to purchasers when you move. A typical Guarantee is the National Housebuilding Council Guarantee (NHBC).

Websites for housebuilders
Most developers have their own websites with details and picture of their developments. These include both new properties and refurbished. In addition there are several websites that specialise in new properties only. One such site is www.newhomesnetwork.co.uk

Buying a Rented House-Right to Buy

If you rent your house from your council, you will be able to buy it at a discount under Right to Buy legislation. the current government has increased discounts in an attempt to increase the right to buy. If you live in a new town, a housing association or housing association trust, you would need to make enquiries, as many are exempt. In order to buy:

- You must have a secure tenancy
- You must have spent at least five years as a tenant of your current landlord or another right to buy landlord
- The house or flat must be a separate dwelling and your only or principle home.

The discount will vary according to length of tenancy and type of property. For further details you should contact your landlord. A scheme, called Statutory Purchase Grant, is also available to assist those tenants of public sector landlords without the right to buy to purchase their homes. The discount is not so generous as the right to buy, usually ranging from £10,000-£13,000. Again details should be obtained from your landlord

Help to Buy Scheme

See chapter 4 for more details on Help to Buy and how it might benefit you.

Shared/part ownership property

There are properties available on a shared/part ownership basis, usually from housing associations. Local Authorities also provide such schemes, although rarely. The main principle is that you buy a percentage of the property, say 50% and you rent the rest, with a service charge if a flat. As time goes by you can "staircase up" to 100% ownership. This is a scheme specially designed for those who cannot meet the full cost of outright purchase in the first instance. Usually, your total monthly outgoings are smaller than they would be if you purchased outright. Social Housing providers run a range of different schemes each year, largely depending on Government requirements. For further details you should contact a large housing association in your area who will provide you with current schemes on offer and point you in the right direction.

Self-build property

Self-build is another option for obtaining a new home. However, it is time consuming and not for the faint hearted. You need to be organised and to have organised the finances and your work programme. Usually the biggest problem is finding a suitable plot of land. There is a lot of competition. It also means that you will, unless you employ an agent, be charged with supervising a number of skilled craftsmen. Self-build usually works out cheaper than buying off a developer but it is certainly not an easy option. For more information and advice check out the following websites:

www.homebuilding.co.uk
This is run by the publishers of homebuilding and renovation magazine which is the leading magazine for homebuilders. The site is magazine style with lots of articles and also a link to www.plotfinder.net. This is a recently established database of land for sale and houses to renovate. There is an annual subscription cost, currently £39.15 (as at 2014/2015)

www.buildstore.co.uk
This site is owned by a group of venture capitalists, individuals and companies involved in the self build market. Again, there is a mix of articles and also adverts.

www.ebuild.co.uk
This site is published by specialist publisher's webguides on line. The site includes a directory of suppliers from architectural salvage to waste disposal with links to useful sites.

www.npbs.co.uk
This is the site of Norwich and Peterborough Building Society, who offer mortgages for self build projects. The loan for self-build is released in stages linked to the building of the property. It is worth checking to see if these mortgages are on offer.

Now read the Key Points from Chapter 1 Overleaf.

Key Points From Chapter One

- When looking for a house, consider essential points such as area and services.

- Think carefully about costs involved and also work if you are considering buying a larger property.

- When purchasing a flat, consider maintenance charges.

- Before viewing, draw up a list of characteristics you will need from a house or flat.

- There are a number of advantages to buying a new house, such as new construction and minimal energy loss.

- Other schemes available include self-build housing

2

The Role of Estate Agents in Buying and Selling Property

Estate Agents

What to expect from an estate agent:

- Advice on the selling or asking price of a house or flat - they know the local market
- Advice on the best way to sell (or buy) and where to advertise; they should discuss an advertising budget with you
- If selling a meeting to visit, assess and value your home and also to take down the particulars of your home. The Property Misdescriptions Act, which arose out of the bad old days of the 1980's, prevents agents from using ambiguous statements to enhance the sale of the property. You should look at the points carefully as people who are disappointed after reading such a glowing report will not purchase.
- They may ask for details of recent bills, such as council tax and electricity. They should also be willing to give advice on fixtures and fittings included in the sale.
- They should be willing to show potential buyers around your home if you are not available.
- Don't expect to have to pay for a for-sale board although some lenders will try to make a charge.

Although a seller does not have any specific duty to disclose information about a property, estate agents have specific legal obligations not to mislead members of the public. Since 2013 agents have been covered by the general duties owed by other businesses to consumers that are set out in the Consumer Protection from Unfair Trading Regulations 2008. These regulations include a ban on misleading statements or omissions and they effectively require estate agents to reveal any material facts about a property to potential buyers.

Choosing an agent if selling

Consider the following points:

- They ought to sell your type of property or specialise in one particular area of the market
- They should be a member of one of the professional bodies such as the National Association of Estate Agents, the Royal Institution of Chartered Surveyors, The Incorporated Society of Valuers and Auctioneers, The Architects and Surveyors Institute or the Association of Building Engineers.
- Obtain quotes of fees, including the basic charge and any extras you might have to pay for, such as advertising in specialist publications.

Choose at least two agents to value the house, if instructing an agent.

Sole agency selling.

Offering an agent sole agency may reduce the fee. This can be done for a limited time. After this you can instruct multiple agents. With sole agency you can sell privately, although you may still be liable for the sole agent's fee.

Joint sole agents

With this arrangement, two or more agents co-operate in the house sale and split the commission. The agents may charge a higher commission in this case.

Multiple agency

This means that you have several agents trying to sell your home, but only pay the agent who sells your property.

The Role of Estate Agents in Buying and Selling Property

Buying property using the internet
There are a number of websites that also detail properties, some are independent and some are owned by the large players.

The following are a selection of the main sites:

www.rightmove.co.uk.
This is one of the largest sites, jointly owned and run by Halifax, Royal Sun Alliance, Connell and Countryside assured Group. They jointly claim to represent more than 170,000 properties covering 99% of UK postcodes. The main function of this site is as a property search site, enabling people to search for property by name of area and postcode.

Each property has a reference number and will have a photo and details. These can be obtained by clicking on the property. There is much useful information, including room sizes.

www.zoopla.co.uk
The claims of this website are that it can help the buyer to find a property, move home and settle in.

www.primelocation.co.uk
This site was launched in 2000 by a consortium of estate agents. This site deals with more expensive properties.

Selling property using the internet
Although estate agents are still the main avenues for selling property, as we have seen, the web now plays a more significant part. In addition to the websites detailed, almost all agents now have their own website. This is really an electronic shop window where your property is displayed. Buyers interested in your property should be able to e-mail the estate agent directly for a viewing.

Now read the key points from chapter 2.

Key points from chapter 2

- Estate agents have a number of roles. However, the main function is to guide the buyer/seller through the process from beginning to end.

- Make sure that you choose the appropriate agent if selling. Make sure that the agent is a member of a professional body.

- You will need to consider whether you wish to sell through more than one estate agent.

- There are a number of websites dealing with buying and selling property. This is often a cheaper way of purchasing or selling.

3

Buying a Property-The Practicalities

Considerations when buying a house or flat

Budget
Before beginning to look for a house you need to sit down and give careful thought to the costs involved in the whole process. The starting point is to identify the different elements in the overall transaction.

Deposit
Sometimes the estate agent will ask you for a small deposit when you make the offer (see Estate Agents, chapter 2). This indicates that you are serious about the offer and is a widespread and legitimate practice, as long as the deposit is not too much, £100 is usual. The main deposit for the property, i.e., the difference between the mortgage and what has been accepted for the property, isn't paid until the exchange of contracts. Once you have exchanged contracts on a property the purchase is legally binding. Until then, you are free to withdraw. The deposit cannot be reclaimed after exchange.

Until recently, and the onset of the recession, banks would normally lend up to 95% of the purchase price of the property. However, particularly now, even though a few banks are willing to lend up to 95% the less you borrow the more favourable terms you can normally get from bank or building society. It has to be said that in the period leading up to the 'credit crunch' we were in a situation where banks loaned money to all and sundry at up to 125% of the value of the home plus exaggerated income multiples. Banks have now tightened up their lending criteria considerably. Recently, The Mortgage Market review came into effect (2014) which has imposed further restrictions on banks and building society lending and requires a stringent set of checks carried out before a mortgage is approved. All lenders insist on larger minimum deposits. This will vary with the bank or building society and you should also scan the Sunday newspapers in particular for details of best buys for mortgages. Refer to the previous chapter for details on help to buy, with the government guaranteeing deposits.

Stamp duty
The following are stamp duty rates as at 2014:

Up to £125,000	Zero
Over £125,000 to £250,000	1%
Over £250,000 to £500,000	3%
Over £500,000 to £1 million	4%
Over £1 million to £2 million	5%
Over £2 million from 22 March 2012	7%
Over £2 million (purchased by certain persons including corporate bodies) from 21 March 2012	15%

Other costs

A solicitor normally carries out conveyancing of property. However, it is perfectly normal for individuals to do their own conveyancing. All the necessary paperwork can be obtained from legal stationers and it is executed on a step-by-step basis. It has to be said that solicitors are now very competitive with their charges and, for the sake of between £600-

£900, it is better to let someone else do the work which allows you to concentrate on other things.

Land Registry

The Land Registry records all purchases of land in England and Wales and is open to the public (inspection of records, called a property search). The registered title to any particular piece of land or property will carry with it a description and include the name of owner, mortgage, rights over other persons land and any other rights. There is a small charge for inspection. A lot of solicitors have direct links and can carry out searches very quickly. Not all properties are registered although it is now a duty to register all transactions. (See chapter 6, conveyancing)

Energy Performance Certificates (EPC's)

EPC's are compulsory. An EPC surveyor will assess the property and looks at all the ways a house or flat can waste heat, such as inadequate loft insulation, lack of cavity wall insulation, draughts and obsolete boilers. After the assessment they will award a rating from A (as good as it gets) to G (terrible). The document also includes information and advice on how to improve matters, such as lagging the water tank or installing double-glazing. An EPC will cost between £120-130 and will be valid for ten years. Improvements made while the certificate is in force will not need a new survey. However, watch out for companies that offer them for higher prices. Always search around.

Structural surveys

The basic structural survey is the homebuyers survey and valuation which is normally carried out by the building society or other lender. This will cost you between £250-£500 and is not really an in-depth survey, merely allowing the lender to see whether they should lend or not, and how much they should lend. Sometimes, lenders keep what they refer to as a retention, which means that they will not forward the full value (less deposit) until certain defined works have been carried out. If you want to go further than a homebuyers report then you will have to instruct a firm

31

of surveyors who have several survey types, depending on how far you want to go and how much you want to spend.

A word of caution. Many people go rushing headlong into buying a flat or house. They are usually exhilarated and wish to complete their purchase fairly quickly in order to establish their new home. If you stop and think about this, it is complete folly and can prove very expensive later. A house or flat is a commodity, like other commodities, except that it is usually a lot more expensive. A lot can be wrong with the commodity that you have purchased which is not immediately obvious. Only after you have completed the deal and paid over the odds for your purchase do you begin to regret what you have done.

The true price of a property is not what the estate agent is asking, certainly not what the seller is asking. The true market price is the difference between what a property in good condition is being sold at and your property minus cost of works to bring it up to that value. Therefore, if you have any doubts whatsoever, and if you can afford it get a detailed survey of the property you are proposing to buy and get the works required costed out. When negotiating, this survey is an essential tool in order to arrive at an accurate and fair price. Do not rest faith in others, particularly when you alone stand to lose.

One further word of caution. As stated, a lot of problems with property cannot be seen. A structural survey will highlight those. In some cases it may not be wise to proceed at all.

Mortgage fees

Mortgage indemnity insurance. This is a one-off payment if you are arranging a mortgage over 70-80% of lenders valuation. This represents insurance taken out by the lender in case the purchaser defaults on payments, in which case the lender will sell the property to reclaim the loan. It is to protect the mortgage lender not the buyer. The cost of the insurance varies depending on how much you borrow. A 90% mortgage on a £60,000 property will cost between £300-600. For a 100% mortgage it is usually much higher. You have to ask yourself, if you are paying up to £2,000 for this kind of insurance on a 100% mortgage, is it not better to try to raise the money to put down a bigger deposit. Always think about the relative economics. A lot of money is made by a lot of people in house buying and selling. The loser is usually the buyer or seller, not the host of middlemen. So think carefully about what you are doing.

Mortgage arrangement fees
Depending upon the type of mortgage you are considering you may have to pay an arrangement fee. You should budget for a minimum of £400.

Buildings insurance
When you have purchased your property you will need to take out buildings insurance. This covers the cost of rebuilding your home if it is damaged. It also covers the cost of subsidence, storm and flood damage, burst pipes and other water leaks and vandalism and third party damage generally. The insurance company will tell you more about elements covered. It is worth shopping around for buildings insurance as prices vary significantly.

Many banks/building societies also supply buildings insurance if you arrange a mortgage with them. You shouldn't immediately take up their offer, as they are not always the most competitive. Websites such as www.confused.com can provide a range of quotes for you.

Removals
Unless you are not moving far and are considering doing it yourself, you should budget for hiring a removal firm. This will depend on how many possessions you have and how much time and money you have. Take care when choosing the removal firm. Choose one who comes recommended if possible. There are other costs too. Reconnection of telephone lines and possibly a deposit, carpets, curtains and plumbing-in washing machines. How much you pay will probably depend on how handy you are yourself. There are also smaller incidental costs such as redirecting mail by the post office. We will be discussing moving home in more depth later on in chapter 8.

Costs of moving

The table below will give you an idea of typical costs, such as solicitors fees, stamp duty, land registry fees and search fees when buying a property. The costs are based on a purchase of a typical London property. Other costs as discussed above will be extra. It has to be stressed that, apart from the stamp duty and Land Registry Fees (which should be checked) solicitor's costs and searches will vary. Searches will cost more in different areas and solicitors fees will come down.

House price	Solicitors fees (av)	Stamp duty	Land Registry	Search fees	Total fees
£150,000	£900	£1500	200	200	2800
£200,000	£900	£1500	200	200	£280
£300,000	£1000	9,000	280	235	10,515
£500,000	£1000	15,000	280	280	16,515
£750,000	1069	30,000	280	280	31,584
£1m	1372	50,000	920	235	52,527
£1.5m	1895	75,000	920	235	73055
£2m	2208	100,000	920	235	103363
£2.5m	2723	175,000	920	235	178,878
£3m	3656	210,000	920	235	214,811
£3.5m	4231	245,000	920	235	246,155
£4m	4871	£280000	920	235	286026

The process of buying a property

Having considered the basic elements of buying a property, the next step is to find the property you want. As we have discussed, this is a long and sometimes dispiriting process. Trudging around estate agents, sorting through mountains of literature, dealing with mountains of estate agents details, scouring the papers and walking the streets! However, most of us find the property we want at the end of the day. It is then that we can put in our offer. One useful way of determining the respective values of property in different areas is to visit a website set up for that purpose www.hometrack.co.uk. This particular site collects price information from selected estate agents in different postcode areas across the country. At the time of writing, prices are currently available for London and the southeast, the southwest, Birmingham and the Midlands and the north of England. Before you decide to look, a little research into prices and comparisons with what you can afford might be useful.

Making an offer

You should put your offer in to the estate agent or direct to the seller, depending who you are buying from.

As discussed earlier, your offer should be based on sound judgement, on what the property is worth not on your desire to secure the property at any cost. A survey will help you to arrive at a schedule of works and cost. If you cannot afford to employ a surveyor from a high street firm then you should try to enlist other help. In addition, you should take a long and careful look at the house yourself, not just a cursory glance. Look at everything and try to get an idea of the likely cost to you of rectifying defects. However, I cannot stress enough the importance of getting a detailed survey. Eventually, you will be in a position to make an offer for the property.

You should base this offer on sound judgement and you should provide a rationalisation for your offer, if it is considerably lower than the asking price. You should make it clear that your offer is subject to contract and survey (if you require further examination or wish to carry out a survey after the offer).

Putting your own home on the market

Most people moving try to secure the sale of their own home before looking for a new one. If you haven't started to sell your house yet, you are advised to do so as soon as possible. You need also to arrange finance. A lot of people have had the nightmarish experience of stepping into an estate agents and being besieged by "independent" financial advisors wishing to sell you their product. Be very careful at this stage. See "getting your mortgage" chapter 5.

Exchange of contracts
Once the buyer and seller are happy with all the details stated in the contract and your conveyancer can confirm that there are no outstanding legal queries, those conveyancing will exchange contracts. The sale is now legally binding for both parties. You should arrange the necessary insurances, buildings and contents from this moment on as you are now responsible for the property.

Buying with a friend
The 1996 Family Law Act brought in the concept of cohabiting couples having the same rights as married couples. This will apply particularly if your marriage starts to break up and you wish to ascertain property rights. However, it is wise to draw up a cohabitation contract prior to purchase which will put in writing how the property is shared and will make clear the situation after break-up. The cohabitation contract can include any conditions you wish and is drawn up usually by a solicitor. There are standard forms for cohabitation agreements which can include financial arrangements stating who pays for the mortgage, who can call for a sale, mutual wills, and who pays for and owns possessions. You can obtain a leaflet concerning this from a Citizens Advice Bureau or from a solicitor.

Completing a sale
This is the final day of the sale and normally takes place around ten days after Exchange. Exchange and completion can take place on the same day if necessary but this is unusual. On day of completion, you are entitled to vacant possession and will receive the keys. See chapter seven for more details on the conveyancing process.

Buying a property in an auction
Property can be purchased in an auction. A small amount are sold in this way. Usually properties sold at auction are either unusual or difficult to put a price on or are repossessions. Auction lists can be obtained from larger estate agents or are advertised in papers. The Estates Gazette, published by the Royal Institute of Chartered Surveyors give details of

auctions in each publication. Normally, this magazine is available to subscribers only although it can be ordered through a newsagent.

Preparing for auction

Because the auction is the final step of the sale, you should have any conveyancing carried out and your mortgage arranged. You will probably need to sell your old home. With this in mind it is a quick way of finding a property if you need to move quite quickly. However, it is likely that your choice of property may be limited and you will need to work on it.

Many properties at auction are sub- standard, this is why they are there in the first place.

You should always do the following:

- Ask for the package compiled by the auctioneer. It will include full details of the property and the memorandum of agreement which is equivalent to the contract.
- View the house
- Organise a conveyancer and instruct him to carry out searches and arrange surveys
- If you like the property, set yourself a price limit to bid to, and arrange a mortgage.

Buying before auction

If the sales details quote "unless previously sold" the seller may be prepared to accept offers before the auction, but he will still accept a fast sale and you will be signing an auction contract. You will need to arrange conveyancing and finance very quickly.

If you are buying at the auction itself, you should remember that the fall of the hammer on your bid is equivalent to the exchange of contracts as for a private sale. You have made a legal arrangement and you will be expected to pay 10-15% deposit on the spot with the remainder of the payment within 28 days.

At the auction

If you are doubtful about your own ability then you can appoint a professional to act on your behalf although they will obviously charge for their services. The seller may be selling subject to a reserve price. If this is the case, it is normally stated in the particulars. The actual figure is not usually disclosed but if the auctioneer states something like "I am going to sell this property today" it is an indication that the reserve price has been reached.

Sale by tender

As an alternative to auction, sale by tender is like a blind auction; you don't know what the other potential buyers are offering. A form of tender is included in the sales details and sometimes sets out the contract details. Always check these details with your conveyancer, because often you cannot pull out after the offer is accepted.

Buyers put their offers in an envelope, sometimes with a 10% deposit. These must be received by the seller's agent at a specified date, at which time the seller will accept one of the offers.

Sale by tender is sometimes used when there have been two or three offers at similar prices.

House swapping

House swapping is an unorthodox but cost effective way of obtaining the property that you are looking for. It is a very efficient way of buying a property. Essentially, you find the property that you want and the seller moves into your house. There is no chain because you are cutting out other buyers. Obviously, the biggest problem is finding someone that you want to swap with and who wants to swap with you.

In practice, the estate agent should be the ideal key player in any swap arrangement. They have a large number of people on their books and who have provided details of their requirements. However, this way of operating seems to be beyond all but the most enterprising estate agencies. In practice, most swaps happen through coincidence.

Saving money through swapping homes

There is a significant saving to be made by swapping homes. If you are the one trading down, for example you have a home worth £275,000 and you want to swap it for a flat worth £150,000, the owner of the flat will be paying for your house with part cash part property. As far as HMRC is concerned this is not a sale on which you would pay stamp duty, but a transfer on which you would pay a notional sum of just £5. However, in this particular type of transaction solicitors must draw up the deal as a single contract with the more expensive property paid partly in kind and partly in cash. You can also save on estate agents fees if you find your swap independently. A useful website dealing with home swaps is: www.home-swap.org.uk. Registration on the site is free.

Now read the key points from Chapter 3.

Key Points From Chapter Three

1 Give careful thought to all the costs of buying property.

2 Some banks lend up to 95% of the purchase price of a property. However, in these straitened times banks are reluctant to lend too much. The more that you lend the more that it costs.

3 If the house or flat costs over £125,000 stamp duty will be payable.

4 You should consider very carefully the need for a full structural survey when buying a property.

5 Always bargain, never offer the asking price.

4

More About Mortgages

Most people purchasing a property will need a mortgage. There are many products on the market and deposits are not always required. However, it is crucial that you are in possession of all the facts when making a decision about a mortgage.

Financial advisers will give you plenty of advice but not always the best advice. Sometimes it is better to go to the lender direct. Before you talk to lenders, work out what your priorities are, such as tax advantage, early repayment and so on. Make sure that you are aware of the costs of life cover.

Lenders-Banks and building societies

There is little or no difference between the mortgages offered by banks and building societies. Because banks borrow against the wholesale money markets, the interest rate they charge to borrowers will fluctuate (unless fixed) as and when their base rate changes. Building societies however, which will rely more heavily on their savers deposits to fund their lending, may adjust the interest rate charged for variable mortgages only once a year. This may be a benefit or disadvantage, depending on whether rates are going up or down.

Centralised lenders

Centralised lenders borrow from the money markets to fund their lending and have no need for the branch network operated by banks and building societies. Centralised lenders, which came to the fore during the 1980s, particularly the house price boom, have been criticised for being quick to implement increases but slow to implement decreases, through rate reductions. This is, simply, because they exist to make profit. Therefore, you should be cautious indeed before embarking on a mortgage with lenders of this kind.

Brokers and "independent" financial advisors

Brokers act as intermediaries between potential borrowers and mortgage providers. If they are "tied" agents they can only advise on the products of one bank, insurance company or building society. If they are independent they should, technically, advise and recommend on every product in the market place.

A word of warning. It is up to you to ask detailed questions about any product a broker offers you. You should ask if they will receive a fee or commission, or both for any sale they arrange for you. Many brokers sell unsuitable products because they receive healthy commissions. In the 1980s it became impossible to enter an estate agents without being forced to enter into discussions with financial advisers who were intent on selling you products which made them a lot of money. If possible, you should arrange a mortgage direct with a bank and avoid so called independent brokers.

How much can you borrow?

There is a standard calculation for working out the maximum mortgage that you will be allowed. For one borrower, three times annual salary, for a joint mortgage, two or two and a half times combined. Lenders, however, will vary and some will lend more. Be very careful not to overstretch yourself. As stated, banks and building societies have tightened up their lending criteria and mortgages are hard to obtain without hefty deposits. At the time of writing, the Financial Conduct Authority have introduced tough new rules to ensure that no one can borrow more than they can afford to repay. These rules represent a further tightening up after the fiasco of the last ten years which has ultimately led to the present crisis. Under the new rules, interest only mortgages will only be offered to people with a firm and clear repayment plan, rather than simply relying on the rise in house prices to cover repayment of the capital. Lenders will also have to take account of future interest rate increases on repayment costs.

Mortgage Market Review

New rules came into force in April 2014 means that those seeking a mortgage should brace themselves for a long wait to see a mortgage adviser, three-hour interviews at the bank and forensic analysis of your daily spending habits.

Even after jumping through all those hoops, success is not guaranteed – experts have warned thousands of buyers and home owners are likely to be rejected because they do not meet the new requirements.

The City regulator, the Financial Conduct Authority (FCA), has introduced the new rules, known as the Mortgage Market Review, to ensure borrowers are issued with mortgages they can afford both now and in the future. The FCA was concerned that lenders were making it too easy to get a mortgage before the financial crisis. Many households borrowed too much money and found they were unable to keep up their repayments when the financial crisis struck.

So-called "self-cert" loans, where borrowers declared their income but did not have to prove or "certify" it, were common and people routinely exaggerated earnings to borrow more. Interest-only loans also caused problems. Borrowers flocked to these deals because their monthly repayments were lower, but they had no way to repay the capital at the end of the loan.

To ensure safer lending in future, mortgage providers are now responsible for assessing whether customers can afford the loan in the long term. This includes buyers and those who are remortgaging and want to increase the size of the loan, vary the time frame or transfer it to a new property.

Deposits

Most banks and building societies used to lend 95% maximum, some more than that. However, for now those days are over. Lenders will usually require higher deposits. The best source of information for reputable lenders is in the weekend newspapers. However, still, the more that you put down the better deal that you are likely to get from the lender.

Help to Buy Scheme
To be eligible for help from Help to Buy, you must:

-Have a deposit of at least 5%;
-Be looking to buy a home worth £600,000 or less;
-Be purchasing a property you intend to live in most of the time;
-This means you can't buy a property you intend to let out or use as a second home.

There are two parts to the scheme - equity loans and mortgage guarantees

Help to Buy scheme - mortgage guarantees
Most of the UK's biggest mortgage lenders have signed up to offer Help to Buy mortgages, as well as smaller lenders.
Help to Buy mortgages work like this:

-You'll put down a deposit of at least 5%
-You can borrow up to 95% of the property's price from a mortgage lender.
-The government will then guarantee any mortgage borrowing above 80% of the property's value.

For example, if you took out a 85% mortgage the government would guarantee to repay your lender up to 10% of its value if you defaulted.
　　But all of this goes on behind the scenes, for you as the borrower it is no different to any other mortgage. You are responsible for repaying the whole loan and could face repossession if you fell into arrears.
　　For the lender, this will mean that lending to people with small deposits will carry much less risk, so it should create much more choice for borrowers. However the government is giving lenders the freedom to set their own interest rates as part of the scheme, so there are no guarantees you'll get an attractive rate.

How equity loans work

A Help to Buy equity loans are only available to people who want to buy a new build property. They work like this:

The government lends you up to 20% of the property's value as an equity loan;

-You'll need a deposit of at least 5%;
-You'll need to get a mortgage of 75% of the property's value.

So if you wanted to buy a house worth £200,000, it would break down as:

-A £40,000 loan from the government;
-A £10,000 deposit put down by you;
-A £150,000 from a mortgage lender.

The benefit to getting an equity loan from the government is that with a larger amount to put down, you'll hopefully get a better mortgage rate from your lender.

Equity loans - what you'll have to pay back

-The equity loan is interest free for the first five years;
-From the sixth year onwards you will pay an admin fee;
-The admin fee will start at 1.75% of the loan;#
-The admin fee will increase every year by any increase in the Retail Prices Index plus 1%.

Remember, you will be paying these fees in addition to your mortgage repayments and the equity loan from the government will not be decreasing in size (unless you opt to repay part of it early). So, over time the cost of the admin fee could become pretty expensive.

You will need to repay the equity loan in full after 25 years, when your mortgage term finishes or when you sell your home - whichever happens first. You will repay the market value of the loan at the time, rather than a fixed cash amount. In practice, this means:

-You take a 20% equity loan to buy a property worth £200,000, or £40,000;
-When you sell the property, it's worth £250,000;
-You repay £50,000 - this is 20% of the new value of your home, not the amount you borrowed;
-If the property had dropped in value, you'd pay less than you borrowed.

You can also choose to repay part of the loan early in chunks of either 10% or 20% of the total value.

Joint mortgages
If you want a joint mortgage, as for any other shared loan you and your partner have a shared responsibility for ensuring that the necessary repayments are made. If something happens to one partner then the other has total responsibility for the loan.

Main types of mortgage
Endowment
With this type of mortgage, you have to take out an endowment insurance policy which is then used to pay off the mortgage loan in a lump sum at the end of the term. There are a number of different types designed to achieve the same end:

- Low cost with profits. This is the usual sort of endowment, guaranteeing to pay back part of the loan only. However, because bonuses are likely to be added, it is usually enough to pay off the loan in full;
- Unit linked endowment. With this, the monthly premiums are used to buy units in investment funds. The drawback is that there is no guarantee how much the policy will be worth on maturity, since this depends on how well the investments have performed.

A word of warning. Endowment products were pushed heavily by financial brokers. There was an obsession with them in the 1980's. This is because they earn big commission for those people that sell them. Like a lot of salespeople, motivated by greed salespeople, some advisers failed to reveal the down side. This is:

-Endowments are investment linked and there is no guarantee that they will have matured sufficiently at the end of the term to repay the mortgage. This leaves you in a mess. A repayment mortgage will definitely have paid off the mortgage at the end of the term. If you change your mortgage and decide that you do not wish to continue with an endowment mortgage, and so cash in the policy early you will almost certainly get a poor return unless it is close to maturity. In the early years of the policy, most of your payments will go towards administration and commission (a fact that your broker does not always reveal). The alternative in these circumstances is to maintain the endowment until it matures, treating it as a stand-alone investment which will, hopefully, make you some money eventually.

Repayment mortgages
This mortgage, where the borrower makes regular repayments to pay the mortgage off over the term is a fairly safe bet. However, if you plan to move house every five years then this will not necessarily be the best mortgage for you. With a repayment mortgage, you pay interest every month but only a small proportion of the capital, particularly in the early years of the mortgage. An endowment mortgage, while more risky, could be better for you under these circumstances, since you can transfer the plan from property to property, while it can, hopefully, grow steadily as it matures.

Pension mortgages
Similar to the other products except that the payments go into a personal pension plan with the remainder after paying the mortgage forming the basis of a pension. The same characteristics apply as to the others.

Interest only mortgage
The borrower pays interest only on the loan, and decides how he or she will pay the loan off at the end. The lender will want to know this too, particularly in the light of the new rules being introduced, mentioned above.

Mixed mortgages
A new development is that one or two lenders now allow borrowers to mix a combination of mortgages in one deal, customising the mortgage to suit each individual.

Foreign currency mortgages
Some foreign banks offer short-term mortgages in the foreign currency of that bank. Their lending criteria can be much more relaxed than trying to borrow from a British lender. The advantage of this sort of mortgage depends on currency fluctuations. If the pound is stable or rises, the borrower benefits. If the pound drops, the borrower will have to pay more. These types of home loans should be left to more sophisticated investors as there is the potential to get into trouble unless you have a clear grasp on the implications of such a mortgage.

Cashbacks
You probably saw the adverts offering large sums of cashback if you took a particular product. If you read the small print, unless you took the highest mortgage available with the highest deposit then you would not get anywhere near such a sum. This mortgage was typical of the many mortgages on offer in the pre-credit crunch times. You would be very hard pushed to see such an offer now.

What to do if you feel that you have been given wrong advice
The mortgage lending market is very complicated and many people have suffered at the hands of financial advisors and others who have given incorrect advice. Mortgage regulation has not been very tight. However, the basic framework is as follows:

- Sales of mortgage linked investments like endowments or pensions are regulated by the Financial Conduct Authority. Anyone selling investments must be qualified and registered and must be able to clearly demonstrate that the policy that they have recommended is suitable. All registered individuals and firms are inspected by regulators and can be fined or expelled from the industry if guilty of wrongly selling products.
- By contrast, information on mortgages is currently regulated by the industry only, voluntarily, under a code of mortgage practice sponsored by the Council of Mortgage Lenders. Although most of the big players are signed up to the code there are still some who are not. Check first before taking advice.

How to complain
- Complain first to the company that sold you the product, going through its internal complaints procedure.
- If you are unhappy with the firm's decision, approach the relevant complaints body. For mortgage advisors employed directly by lenders, or complaints about lenders generally, contact the Financial Ombudsman Service on 0300 123 9 123 or www.financial-ombudsman.org.uk
- For mortgage lenders which are not building societies or banks but which are signed up to the mortgage code, the Chartered Institute of Arbitrators 020 7421 7455 www.ciarb.org will assist.
- If your complaint is about a mortgage broker, contact the Chartered Institute of Arbitrators which may be able to help if the firm is registered under the code.
- Complaints about endowments, pensions and other investments is handled by the Financial Conduct Authority 0800 111 67 68 www.fca..org.uk and are dealt with by the financial ombudsman Service.

The most common complaint is to do with endowments. A lot of people bought products which they came to regret. They are a major source of profit to the provider-and all those in between-but the person left holding the problem is the consumer.

If you believe that you have been given bad advice about anything to do with the insurance or investment side of a product then you should approach the Financial Services Authority.

The Building Society Association or the British Bankers Association have free publications that should help you. In addition, the Consumers Association, "Which" runs regular articles on mortgages. Remember - always ask questions. Never rush into anything. Always take advice if you are uncertain. Banks and building societies themselves are usually a better source, a safer source than individual advisers.

Borrowing and the internet
Almost all lenders have their own sites and many operate internet only loans with keener rates than those available on the high street. But there are also growing numbers of mortgage broker sites, offering mortgage calculators so that you can work out how much you can afford to borrow and how much the true cost of your loan will be.

The following are a selection of independent sites:

www.moneysupermarket.co.uk
This is an online mortgage broker with a choice of over 4000 variable, fixed rate, capped and discounted mortgages as well as more specialist loans for right to buy, buy to let and self build property, also self certification loans.

www.moneynet.co.uk
This is an independent on line mortgage broker, offering mortgages from over 100 lenders. Again, as with all these sites it will provide a clear and comprehensive picture of mortgages available and is easy to use, just follow the instructions.

www.moneyextra.co.uk

An independent financial advisor with access to over 4500 products including all kinds of mortgages for all types of client.

Now read the Key Points from Chapter Four overleaf.

****

Key Points From Chapter Four

1   There are many mortgage products on the market. Choose carefully. Understand advice- make sure all is clear.

2   The more you borrow, the more you pay at the outset and over the term.

3   If you are given wrong advice or feel aggrieved in any way there are mechanisms for complaint.

5

Selling Your Home

Estate agents
Ask for quotes from at least three agents before instructing one or more of them. The fee is normally based on the selling price of the house and is between 1 - 3 per cent of the final selling price. However, VAT (currently 20%) will be added on to this. The next chapter on conveyancing gives an idea of the processes involved once a buyer is found.

DIY Selling
If you want to save the cost of instructing an agent to sell your house, you could try to sell it yourself. Around 4 - 5% of homes in the UK are sold privately. There are a number of useful guides which are dedicated to this subject. One site worth visiting is www. uknetguide.co.uk.

Setting the price if selling yourself
You need to see how much similar properties are sold for in the area. If this proves difficult, get a professional valuation. See Yellow Pages under Surveyors or Valuers or contact the Royal Institution of Chartered Surveyors. A valuation report will only value and will not assess structural soundness. A survey is needed for that. Put together the sales particulars in the same way that an estate agent would. It is advisable to put a disclaimer on these details such as "these particulars are believed to be accurate and are set out as a general outline only for the guidance of interested buyers. They do not constitute, nor constitute parts of, an offer or contract.

Advertising your property independently
There are a number of ways you can advertise your property. Local papers will advertise for you and also there are free ad papers. In addition, there are a number of companies with a computerised sales

network who will charge you a flat fee for advertising. Be accurate with the details - you may leave yourself open to damages through misrepresentation. If an offer is made to you then you should then hand matters over to your solicitor.

As discussed, some sellers handle their own conveyancing lock stock and barrel. This includes the legal side. However, this book cannot advise you on legal conveyancing. That is a separate matter. Suffice to say that it follows a standard format. It is easier, in the light of the reduced prices available to appoint a solicitor to do this side for you.

Selling at Auction

Advantages of auction

An auction is an efficient and cost effective way of selling property and if prepared properly with intensive marketing, advertising and mailing, will result in the greatest possible exposure of the lots offered. To maximize the effectiveness of the marketing, considerable thought must be given to the guide price, which needs to be tailored to generate competitive bidding in the auction room, thus ensuring that the best price is being achieved. Although some properties are more suitable for sale by private treaty, taking this route does present uncertainties over terms such as sale price and timing of exchange and completion.

Selling by auction however, offers a high degree of certainty that a sale will be achieved on a given day and, significantly, on the fall of the gavel an immediate binding contract is formed. As no further negotiation is permitted the entire sale process, from instruction to exchange of contracts can be, is achieved within as little as six to eight weeks.

For vendors with a large number of properties to sell, auctions provide a highly efficient method of sale allowing for a total or phased disposal programme selling in individual lots thus maximising receipts. For those selling in a fiduciary capacity, there is the added advantage of the sale being entirely open and transparent. Most types of property are suitable for auction provided that a realistic reserve price is agreed.

Who sells at auction?

Auction is now regarded as the optimum method of sale for many sellers who range from private investors and property companies to banks, housing associations and local authorities.

When do you want to sell?

Decide when you want to sell your property and which auction you would like to put it in. Sale dates and venues can be found on auctioneers websites.

What information do auctioneers need?

In order to give you the best possible advice auctioneers will need the following details:

Address
Description
Photograph
Tenure and Tenancy (if applicable) details
Floor plan or site plan
Anything else you consider to be material

Once the auctioneers have received this information, they will provide an estimate of the likely sale price of your property at Auction. Together with a proposed reserve, they shall send you a copy of their standard agency contract setting out their terms and conditions. Once the maximum reserve price is agreed you will be asked to sign and return the standard agency contract to confirm your instructions, at which time the Entry Fee becomes payable.

Proof of identity

If an auctioneer has not sold for you before they will require proof of your identity and address before they can market your property.

Auction Entry Fee

All auctioneers will charge a fee to enter a property into an auction. This fee is payable whether the property is sold or not. The fee is a contribution towards the cost of marketing and catalogue production. The fee will depend on how much space is taken in the catalogue for the property.

Commission

In the event of a sale, an auctioneer's commission is up to 2% of the sale price plus VAT for a sole agency or 2.5% plus VAT for a joint agency. A joint agency is usually advisable where the auctioneer feels it is necessary to include a local estate agent to handle local enquiries and conduct viewing. The auction house surveyors will confirm the auction entry fee and commission rate with you in writing before accepting your instructions.

Sales particulars

Once the auctioneer has been formally instructed, the property will be inspected by one of their surveyors, measurements taken where appropriate, and the property will be photographed. Draft sales particulars will then be forwarded to you and to your solicitors for approval and/or amendments.

Legal documents

At the same time your solicitors will be instructed to prepare a legal pack containing special conditions of sale, title documents, leases (where applicable), searches, planning documentation and office copy entries so that they are available to interested parties either by post or on line.

Guide price

The auction team will recommend a guide price which you will need to approve before marketing begins. It is important to set the guide price at a realistic level which is attractive to buyers. This will generate competitive bidding in the auction room and ensure that best value is achieved.

Marketing your property

Marketing will usually start approximately three to four weeks prior to the auction sale. Auction Houses produce thousands of catalogues for each auction. These are sent to prospective buyers such as private investors, property companies and developers. Catalogues are also available online and auctioneers send regular email alerts to the private investors who are registered on the site.

Advertising and PR

Good auctioneers will advertise in the key property publications and place advertisements in local newspapers.

Targeted Marketing

Auction houses also target individuals who have previously expressed an interest in similar properties, as well as adjacent occupiers, local agents, local developers, builders and property companies.

Viewings and Surveys

Potential purchasers may want to view your property during the marketing period and have a survey carried out. You should let the auctioneer know how you would prefer viewings to be arranged and we shall arrange access for buyers. In most cases, vacant properties are open at pre-arranged times for viewing. Details will be printed in the catalogue.

Legal documentation

In conjunction with your solicitors the auction house will supply copy documents to prospective purchaser's solicitors and will keep you constantly updated as to the levels of interest shown.

The reserve price

The auction House will agree a reserve price with you for your property a few days before the auction. This is the level below which they will not be authorised to sell. It is important that this be set at a realistic level.

Auction day
The Fall of the Gavel
On the fall of the Auctioneer's gavel, a binding contract is effected. The successful bidder is required to provide the name, address and telephone number of the purchaser and the purchaser's solicitors. The successful bidder will also be asked to provide a deposit for 10% of the purchase price. Identification of the purchaser is always checked at this stage. Clearance of all deposit cheques is arranged immediately after the auction.

Exchange of Contracts
The Memorandum of Sale is made up in the room and given to the purchaser to sign. The exchange is overseen by the auction house's solicitor. They will forward the purchaser's signed Memorandum of Sale to your solicitor. Completion will usually, take place 20 working days later. The deposit funds are then paid to you less fees.

What happens if the property does not sell on the day?
If your property fails to reach its reserve in the room, someone may still wish to buy it. You will need to decide whether to accept any offer and advise the auction house accordingly. The property may even be sold in the days or weeks after the sale as we continue to market the property.

Quick Results
The entire process, from instruction to exchange of contracts, can be achieved within as little as six to eight weeks.

Now read the key points from Chapter 5.

Key points from Chapter Five

- Ask for quotes from at least three agents before agreeing to sell

- You could try to sell your property yourself. Internet selling is becoming more popular

- It is important to get an accurate valuation before selling

- Selling by auction is one route of sale if your property is proving hard to sell

6

Conveyancing a Property

Conveyancing, or the practice of conveyancing, is about how to transfer the ownership of land and property from one person or organisation to another. Land and property can include freehold property, leasehold property (residential) or can include business leases. *Essentially, the process of conveyancing lays down clear procedures for the conveyancer and also sets out each party's position during the sale or acquisition.*

Before understanding the process of conveyancing, however, it is essential to understand something about the legal forms of ownership of property.

Legal ownership of property

There are two main forms of legal ownership of property in Great Britain. If you are about to embark on the sale or acquisition of a house or flat (or business) then you will be dealing in the main with either freehold or leasehold property.

It is very rare indeed to find other forms of ownership, although the government has introduced a form of ownership called 'common hold' that in essence creates the freehold ownership of flats, with common responsibility for communal areas.

Freehold property

In general, if you own the freehold of a house or a piece of land, then you will be the outright owner with no fixed period of time and no one else to answer to (with the exception of statutory authorities).

There may be registered restrictions on title, which will be discussed later. The property will probably be subject to a mortgage so the only other overriding interest will be that of the bank or the building society. The responsibility for repairs and maintenance and general upkeep will be the freeholders. The law can intervene if certain standards are not maintained. The deed to your house will be known as the "freehold transfer document" which will contain any rights and obligations. Usually, the transfer document will list any "encumbrances" (restrictions) on the use of the land, such as rights of way of other parties, sales restrictions etc. The deeds to your home are the most important documentation. As we will see later, without deeds and historical data, such as the root of title, it can be rather complicated selling property. This is why the system of land registration in use in this country has greatly simplified property transactions.

Any person owning freehold property is free to create another interest in land, such as a lease or a weekly or monthly tenancy, subject to any restrictions the transfer may contain.

Leasehold property

If a person lives in a property owned by someone else and has an agreement for a period of time, usually a long period, over 21 years and up to 99 years or 125 years, in some cases 999 years, then they are a leaseholder.

The conveyancing of leasehold property is, potentially, far more problematic than freehold property, particularly when the flat is in a block with a number of units. The lease is a contract between landlord and tenant which lays down the rights and obligations of both parties and should be read thoroughly by both the leaseholder and, in particular, the conveyancer. Once signed then the purchaser is bound by all the clauses in the contract. It is worth taking a little time looking at the nature of a lease before discussing the rather more complex process of conveyancing. Again, it has to be stated that it is of the utmost importance that both the purchaser and the vendor understand the nature of a lease.

The lease
Preamble
The start of a lease is called the preamble. This defines the landlord and purchaser and also the nature of the property in question (the demise). It will also detail the remaining period of the lease.

Leaseholders covenants

Covenants are best understood as obligations and responsibilities. Leaseholder's covenants are therefore a list of things that leaseholders should do, such as pay their service charges and keep the interior of the dwelling in good repair and not to, for example, alter the structure. The landlord's covenants will set out the obligations of the landlord, which is usually to maintain the structure and exterior of the block, light common parts etc.

One unifying theme of all leasehold property is that, notwithstanding the landlord's responsibilities, it is the leaseholder who will pay for everything out of a service charge.

Leases will make detailed provisions for the setting, managing and charging of service charges, which should include a section on accounting. All landlords of leaseholders are accountable under the Landlord and Tenant Act 1985, as amended. These Acts will regulate the way a landlord treats a leaseholder in the charging and accounting of service charges.

In addition, the 1996 Housing Act, as amended by the 2002 Commonhold and Leasehold Reform Act has provided further legislation protecting leaseholders by introducing the right of leaseholders to go to Leasehold Valuation Tribunals if they are unhappy with levels and management of charges and also to carry out audits of charges. It is vital that, when buying a leasehold property that you read the lease. Leases tend to be different from each other and nothing can be assumed. When you buy a property, ensure that the person selling has paid all debts and has contributed to some form of "sinking fund" whereby provision has been built up for major repairs in the future. Make sure that you will not be landed with big bills after moving in and that, if you are, there is money to deal with them. After a lease has been signed then there is little or no recourse to recoup any money owed.

These are all the finer points of leases and the conveyancer has to be very vigilant. In particular read the schedules to the lease as these sometimes contain rather more detail.

One of the main differences between leasehold and freehold property is that the lease is a long tenancy agreement which contains provisions which give the landlord rather a lot of power to manage (or mismanage) and it is always a possibility that a leaseholder can be forced to give up his or her home in the event of non compliance with the terms of the lease. This is known as forfeiture.

Under legislation referred to earlier, a new 'no fault right to manage' has been introduced. This enables leaseholders who are unhappy with the management of their property, to take over the management with relative ease. The Act applies to most landlords, with the exception of Local Authorities. These powers go a long way to curb the excesses or inefficiencies of numerous landlords and provide more control and greater security for leaseholders.

Check points
There are key areas of a lease that should be checked when purchasing.

- What is the term left on the lease?
- Is the preamble clear, i.e. is the area which details landlord, tenant and demised (sold) premises, clear?
- Is the lease assignable- i.e. can you pass on the lease without landlords permission or does it need surrendering at sale or a license to assign?
- What is the ground rent and how frequently will you pay it?
- What is the level of service charge, if any, and how is it collected, apportioned, managed and accounted for?
- What are the general restrictions in the lease, can you have pets for example, can you park cars and do you have a designated space?
- What are the respective repairing obligations? As we have seen, the leaseholder will pay anyway but the landlord and leaseholder will hold respective responsibilities. This is an important point because occasionally, there is no stated responsibility for upkeep and the environment deteriorates as a consequence, diminishing the value of the property.

Two systems of conveyancing
After gaining an understanding of the nature of the interest in land that you are buying, it is absolutely essential to understand the two systems of conveyancing property in existence, as this will determine, not so much the procedure because the initial basic steps in conveyancing, such as carrying out searches, are common to both forms of land, registered and unregistered, but the way you go about the process and the final registration.

Registered and unregistered land
In England and Wales the method of conveyancing to be used in each particular transaction very much depends on whether the land is *registered* or *unregistered* land. If the title, or proof of ownership, of land and property has been registered under the Land Registration Acts 1925-86 then the Land Registry (see below) will be able to furnish the would-be conveyancer with such documentation as is required to establish ownership, third party rights etc. If the land has not been registered then proof of ownership of the land in question must be traced through the title deeds.

Registered land
As more and more conveyancing is falling within the remit of the Land Registry, because it is compulsory to register land throughout England and Wales, it is worth outlining this system briefly at this stage.

The Land Registration Acts of 1925 established the Land Registry (HM Land Registry). The Land Registry is a department of the Civil Service, at its head is the Chief Land Registrar. All applications to the Land Registry must be made within the district in question.

There is a specific terminology in use within conveyancing, particularly within the land registry:
a) *a piece of land*, or parcel of land is known as a *registered title*
b) the owner of land is referred to as the *registered proprietor*
c) a conveyance of registered land is called *a transfer*
d) a transaction involving registered land is known as *a dealing*

The main difference between the two types of conveyancing *registered* and *unregistered* concerns what is known *as proof of title*. In the case of land that is unregistered the owner will prove title by showing the would-be purchaser the documentary evidence which shows how he or she came to own the land and property.

In the case of registered land the owner has to show simply that he or she is registered at the Land Registry as the registered proprietor. Proof of registration is proof of ownership, which is unequivocal. In registered land the documents proving ownership are replaced by the fact of registration. Each separate title or ownership of land has a title number, which the Land Registry uses to trace ownership, or confirm ownership. The description of each title on the register is identified by the *title number,* described by reference to the filed plan (indicating limits and extent of ownership). With registered conveyancing the Land Registry keeps the register of title and file plan and title. The owner (proprietor) is issued with a Land Certificate. If the land in question is subject to a mortgage then the mortgagee is issued with a Land Certificate.

Production of the Land Certificate
With registered land, whenever there is a sale, or disposition, then the Land Certificate must be produced to the Land Registry in the appropriate district. If proved that a Certificate is lost or destroyed then a new one can be issued by the Land Registry.

The key steps in the process of conveyancing property
Before the buyer exchanges contracts on a property, whether registered or unregistered, and then completes the purchase a number of searches are always carried out. These are:

Enquiry's before contract
Local land charges search
Enquiry's of the local authority
Index map search
The above searches will now be carried out by the seller, or by the agent

acting for the seller, prior to marketing the property through the HIP. These are the most essential and common searches.

Making enquiry's before contract

These are enquiry's to the seller, or the Vendor of the property and are aimed at revealing certain facts about the property that the seller has no legal obligation to disclose to the buyer. There are certain matters, which are always raised. These are:

a) Whether there are any existing boundary disputes
b) What services are supplied to the property, whether electricity, gas or other
c) Any easements or covenants in the lease. These are stipulations in the lease, which give other certain rights, such as rights of way.
d) Any guarantees in existence

Planning considerations
a) Adverse rights affecting the property
b) Any fixtures and fittings
c) Whether there has been any breach of restriction affecting the property

If the property is newly built, information will be required concerning any outstanding works or future guarantees of remedying defects. Where a property is leasehold, information will be required about the lessor.

Registered conveyancers will use a standard form to raise these enquiry's, so that the initial search is exhaustive. As part of the move towards openness in the process of buying and selling property, and also an attempt to speed up the process of sale, the Law Society has introduced new forms which the solicitor, or buyer if carrying out his or her own conveyancing, is being encouraged to use. These are Seller's Property Information Forms relating to freehold and leasehold property, that the seller and solicitor will respectively fill in, a form relating to fixtures, fittings and contents and a form relating to complete information and requisitions on title.

These forms can be obtained from a legal stationers, such as Oyez and have the pre-fix Prop 1-7.

If a conveyancer is being used then it is advisable to ask whether or not they are using these newly introduced forms. The main point is that you should think long and hard about the type of questions that should be raised. The vendor does not have to answer the questions, but beware a vendor who refuses to disclose answers. Answers given by the vendor do not form part of the subsequent contract and therefore cannot be used against that person in the event of future problems. However, the Misrepresentations Act of 1976 could be evoked if a deliberate misrepresentation has caused problems.

Local land charges search

The Local Land Charges Act 1975 requires District Councils, London Borough Councils and the City of London Corporation to maintain a Local Land Charges Registry for the area. Local land charges can be divided into two areas:

a) Financial charges on the land for work carried out by the local authority
b) restrictions on the use of land

The register is further divided into twelve parts:

a) general financial charges
b) specific financial charges
c) planning charges
d) miscellaneous charges and provisions
e) charges for improvements of ways over fenland
f) land compensation charges
g) new town charges
h) civil aviation charges
i) open cast coal mining charges
j) listed buildings charges

k) light obstruction notices
l) drainage scheme charges

All charges are enforceable by the local authority except g and i, which are enforced by statutory bodies and private individuals generally. A buyer should search in all parts of this particular register and this can be done by a personal or official search. A personal search, as the name suggests, involves the individual or their agent attending at the local authority office and, on paying the relevant fee, personally searching the register. The charges are registered against the land concerned and not against the owner. The official search is the one most favored because, in the event of missing a vital piece of information the chances of compensation are far higher than with a personal search.

With the official search a requisition for a search and for an official certificate of search is sent to the Registrar of Local Land Charges for the area within which the land is situated. There is a fee and the search is carried out by the Registrars staff, which results in a certificate being sent to the person making the request, which clearly outlines any charges. The Registrar may require a plan of the land as well as the postal address. Separate searches are made of each parcel of land being purchased.

Local authority searches

There is a standard form in use for these particular types of searches. This is known as "Con 29 England and Wales" Revised April 2000, with the format of the form differing slightly for inner London boroughs. Any of the forms in the process can be obtained from legal stationers.

The standard forms in use contain a statement to the effect that the local authority is not responsible for errors unless negligence is proved. Many of the enquiries relate specifically to planning matters, whilst other elements of the search are concerned about roads and whether they are adopted and whether there are likely to be any costs falling onto property owners. We will be considering planning matters concerning the individual property a little later. Other enquiry's relate to possible construction of new roads which may affect the property, the location of sewers and pipes and whether the property is in an area of compulsory registration of title, a smoke control area or slum clearance area. The form used is so constructed that part 2 of the form contains questions, which must be initialled by the purchaser before they are answered. Again these questions cover planning and other matters. Other enquiry's can be asked by the individual, which are answered at the authorities discretion. In addition to the above, which are the major searches, there are others that the conveyancer has to be aware of. These are as follows:

Searches in the Index map and parcels index of the Land register
If the land has been registered the title will be disclosed and whether it is registered leasehold or freehold. Registered rent charges are also disclosed by the search. (See chapter 7.)

Commons Registration Act (1965) search
This act imposes a duty on County Councils to keep a register relating to village greens and common land and interests over them, such as right of way.

Coal mining search
The request for this search if relevant, is designed to reveal the whereabouts of mineshafts and should be sent to the local Area Coal Board office, or its equivalent. The search will disclose past workings and any subsidence, proposed future workings and the proximity of opencast workings. It is usually well known if there is a problem, or potential problem with coal mining in an area and this search is essential if that is the case.

Other enquiry's
There are a number of other bodies from which it might be appropriate to request a search. These include British Rail, statutory undertakers such as electricity and gas boards, planning authorities generally, rent assessment committees and so on. These will only usually be necessary if there is a direct link between the property being purchased and a particular circumstance within an area or property.

Planning matters relating to specific properties

It is obviously very necessary to determine whether or not any illegal alterations have been carried out to the property you wish to purchase, before reaching the point of exchange of contracts. This is to ensure that the vendor has complied with relevant planning legislation, if any material changes have been made, and that you will not be required at a later date to carry out remedial work. The Local Authority maintains a register of planning applications relating to properties within their boundaries. In addition, the register will also reveal any planning enforcement notices in force against a particular property.

Questions such as these, and also any questions relating to the effect of Structure or Local plans, (specific plans relating to local and borough wide plans for the future) should be made in writing to the local authority or an individual search can be carried out. Usually they are carried out if there is any suspicion that planning regulations may have been breached.

In addition, there may be other considerations, such as whether the building is listed or whether tree preservation orders relating to trees within the cartilage of the property are in force. It is certainly essential to know about these. It is highly recommended that all of these searches are carried out and completed before contracts are exchanged.

The contract for sale

As with many other transactions, a sale of land is effected through a contract. However, a contract, which deals with the sale of land, is governed by the requirements of the Law of Property (miscellaneous provisions) Act 1989, the equitable doctrine of specific performance and the duty of the vendor to provide title to the property.

The Law of Property Act (Miscellaneous provisions) 1988 provides that contracts dealing with the sale of land after 26th September 1989 must be in writing. The contract must contain all the terms and agreements to which the respective parties to the transaction have agreed. The provisions of the Act do not apply to sales at a public auction, contracts to grant a short lease and contracts regulated under the Financial Services Act 1986. If the person purchasing is doing so through an agent then the agent must have authority to act on behalf of the purchaser. Examples of agents are auctioneers and solicitors, also estate agents. If the phrase "subject to contract" is used in a sale then the intention of both parties to the contract is that neither are contractually bound until a formal contract has been agreed by the parties, signed and exchanged. Therefore, the words "subject to contract" are a protective device, although it is not good to depend on the use of these words throughout a transaction

Procedures in the formation of contract

The vendor's solicitor will usually draw up an initial contract of sale. This is because only this person has access to all the necessary initial documents to begin to effect a contract. The draft contract is prepared in two parts and sent to the purchaser's solicitor (if using a solicitor), the other side will approve or amend the contract as necessary. Both sides must agree to any proposed amendments. After agreement has been reached, the vendor's solicitor will retain one copy of the contract and send the other copy to the solicitor or person acting for the other side. The next stage is for the vendors solicitor to engross (sign and formalise) the contract in two parts. Both parts are then sent to the purchaser's solicitor or other agent who checks that they are correct then sends one part back to the vendor's solicitor.

The Contents of a contract

A contract will be in two parts, *the particulars of sale* and the *conditions of sale*. The particulars of sale give a physical description of the land and also of the interest, which is being sold. A property must be described accurately and a plan may be attached to the contract to emphasize or illustrate what is in the contract. The particulars will also outline whether the property is freehold or leasehold and what kind of lease the vendor is assigning, i.e., head lease (where vendor is owner of the freehold) or underlease, where the vendor is not.

It is very important to determine what kind of lease it is that is being assigned, indeed whether it is assignable or whether permission is needed from the landlord and it is recommended that a solicitor handle this transaction. This is because any purchaser of a lease can find his or her interest jeopardized by the nature of the lease. Where a sub-lease, or under lease is being purchased, the purchasers interest can be forfeited by the actions of the head lessee, the actions of this person being out of control of the purchaser.

Rights, such as easements and also restrictive covenants, which are for the benefit of the land, should be expressly referred to in the particulars of sale. In addition, the vendor should refer to any latent defects affecting his or her property, if known. This includes any encumbrances, which may affect the property.

Misdescription

If the property in the particulars of sale is described wrongly, i.e. there is a mis-statement of fact, such as describing leasehold as freehold land, calling an under-lease a lease or leaving out something that misleads the buyer, in other words, if the misdescription is material, then the purchaser is entitled to rescind the contract. Essentially the contract must describe what is being sold and if it does not, and the buyer is mislead then the contract is inaccurate. If the misdescription is immaterial and insubstantial, and there has been no misrepresentation then the purchaser cannot rescind the contract. However, if the misdescription has affected the purchase price of the property then the purchaser can insist on a reduction in the asking price. The purchaser should claim this compensation before completion takes place. The vendor has no right to rescind the contract if the misdescription is in the purchaser's favour, for example, the area of land sold is greater than that intended. Neither can the vendor compel the purchaser to pay an increased purchase price

Misrepresentation

Misrepresentation is an untrue statement of fact made by one party or his or her agent, which induces the other party to enter into the contract. An opinion and a statement of intention must be distinguished from a statement of fact. There are three types of misrepresentation, fraudulent misrepresentation, negligent misrepresentation and innocent misrepresentation. Fraudulent misrepresentation is a false statement made knowingly or without belief in its truth, or recklessly. The innocent party may sue through the tort of negligence either before or after the contract is complete and rescind the contract. Negligent misrepresentation, although not fraudulent, is where the vendor or his or her agents cannot prove that the statement they made in relation to the contract was correct. Remedies available are damages or rescission of the contract. Innocent misrepresentation is where the statement made was neither fraudulently or negligently but is still an untrue statement. Rescission is available for this particular type of misrepresentation. Rescission of contract generally is available under the Misrepresentation Act 1967 s 2(2).

Non-disclosure
Generally, in the law of contract, there is the principle of "caveat emptor" "let the buyer beware". In other words, it is up to the purchaser to ensure that what he or she is buying is worth the money paid for it. Earlier we talked about the importance of searches and also, particularly, the importance of the structural survey. Although the vendor has some responsibility to reveal any defects in the property it is always very advisable for the purchaser to ensure that all checks prior to purchase are carried out thoroughly.

Signing the contract
The vendors solicitor will obtain the vendors signature to the contract, when he is satisfied that the vendor can sell what he is purporting to do through the contract. The purchaser's solicitor or agent will do the same, having checked the replies to all enquiry's before contract. It is also essential to check that a mortgage offer has been made and accepted.

Exchanging contracts
Neither party to the sale is legally bound until there has been an exchange of contracts. At one time, a face to face exchange would have taken place.

However, with the rapid increases in property transactions this rarely happen nowadays. Exchange by post is more common. The purchaser will post his or her part of the contract together with the appropriate cheque to cover the agreed deposit, to the purchaser's solicitor or person acting on behalf of that Person. The purchaser's solicitor will usually insert the agreed completion date. On receiving this part of the contract the vendor will add his or her part and send this off in exchange. At this stage, both parties become bound under the contract.

A contract to convey or create an estate in land is registrable as a class C (IV) land charge, an estate contract. You should take further advice on this, as it is not current practice to do so.

Completion

The requirements concerning completion are detailed thoroughly in the general conditions of sale. Payment on completion is one such detail. Payment on completion should be by one of the following methods:

a) legal tender;
b) bankers draft;
c) an unconditional authority to release any deposit by the stakeholder
d) any other method agreed with the vendor.

At common law, completion takes place whenever the vendor wishes and payment is to be made by legal tender. Also dealt with in the general conditions is failure to complete and notices to complete. Failure to complete can cause difficulty for one of the other parties and the aggrieved party can serve notice on the other to complete by a specific date. The notice has the effect of making "time of the essence" which means that a specific date is attached to completion, after which the contract is discharged.

Return of pre-contract deposits

The vendor must return any deposit paid to the purchaser if the purchaser drops out before the exchange of contracts. This cannot be prevented and was the subject of a House of Lords ruling.

The position of the parties after exchange of contracts

Once a contract has been exchanged, the purchaser is the beneficial owner of the property, with the vendor owning the property on trust for the purchaser. The vendor is entitled to any rents or other profits from the land during this period, has the right to retain the property until final payments have been made and has a lien (charge/right) over the property in respect of any unpaid purchase monies.

The vendor is bound to take reasonable care of the property and should not let the property fall into disrepair or other damages to be caused during the period between exchange and completion. If completion does not take place at the allotted time and the fault is the purchasers then interest can be charged on the money due.

The purchaser, as beneficial owner of the property is entitled to any increase in the value of the land and buildings but not profits arising. The purchaser has a right of lien over the property, the same as the vendor, in respect of any part of the purchase price paid prior to completion.

Bankruptcy of the vendor

In the unfortunate event of the vendor going bankrupt in between exchange and completion, the normal principles of bankruptcy apply so that the trustee in bankruptcy steps in to the vendor's shoes. The purchaser can be compelled to complete the sale. The trustee in bankruptcy is obliged to complete the sale if the purchaser tenders the purchase money on the completion day.

Bankruptcy of the purchaser

When a purchaser is declared bankrupt in between sale and completion all of his or her property vests in the trustee in bankruptcy. In these circumstances, the vendor can keep any deposit due to him.

Death of Vendor or purchaser

The personal representatives of a deceased vendor can compel the purchaser to sell. The money is conveyed to those representatives who will hold the money in accordance with the terms of any will or in accordance with the rules relating to intestacy if there is no will.

The same position applies to the purchaser's representatives, who can be compelled by the vendor to complete the purchase and who can hold money on the purchaser's behalf.

Now read the key points from chapter 6

Key Points From Chapter 6

- Conveyancing is about the practice of transferring a property from one to another.

- There are two main types of property ownership in Britain-Freehold and leasehold

- The lease is the single most important document if buying leasehold

- There are two systems of conveyancing – registered and unregistered.

- The contract of sale must be scrutinised thoroughly before exchange and completion

7

Planning Moving Arrangements

At this stage, you will either have sold your home and /or be ready to move into a new one. The process of moving home is closely linked with the completion of the purchase of another home. That is, assuming that you are moving to another bought property. Of course, you may be moving to a rented home.

However you choose to time your move, there are certain core tasks, as follows:

- Finalise removal and storage arrangements
- Contact electricity/gas/phone/cable companies and any other relevant company to tell them your moving date
- Organise your funds so that you can transfer all remaining money needed to complete the sale into your solicitors account for him/her to pay the sellers solicitor

One main question is: do you get a removal firm or do you do it yourself?

DIY moves
This is cheaper than hiring a removal company, especially if you have a few possessions or no big items of furniture. You will also need willing and able friends. However, do not take the decision to move yourself lightly. Think carefully about the amount of furniture that you have and the fact that your house may be a particularly difficult site to move from.

Using professionals
Professionals know what they are doing and can leave you to organise all the other aspects of moving whilst they do the donkey work. This may cost you more money. However, it may be well worth it. Use a firm which is a

member of the British Association of Removers (www.bar.co.uk). Members of this body have to adhere to a code of professional practice, meet minimum standards and provide emergency service and finance guarantees.

Removers can offer various levels of packing services. The most expensive option is for the remover to pack everything. The second most expensive option is for them to pack the breakable things such as glass. The cheapest way is for the removers to provide crates and for you to do your own packing.

If you are going for the professional option:

- Get two or three estimates. You can find the names of local firms through the British Association of Removers, through the yellow pages (www.yell.com) or through Thomson's Directories (www.thomweb.co.uk)
- There are a growing number of websites that include quotes from removal firms (see below)
- You should expect estimators to go through your whole property including gardens and loft
- Check whether your possessions will be covered by your household insurance policy and extend the cover if they are not
- Don't wait to exchange contracts to organise removers.

The following Websites may be useful:
www.reallymoving.com
This site was launched in 1999 and is the leading provider of online removal services. Registering on the site will get you three quotes from removers. It also covers solicitors, surveyors and others involved in the buying and selling process.

Contacting utilities
A boring but essential task is to contact all of the companies that provide you with services to tell them that you have moved. This should be done

after you exchange contracts, obtaining meter readings etc. Most utilities will ask you for confirmation of your new address and moving date in writing. If you cannot face this task then use the following website:

www.iammoving.com

This site was started in 1999 by a consortium of investors and industry figures. The claim is to be the UK's first free online change of address service. You register, enter your old and new address, supply account numbers and meter readings where relevant and iammoving will send the information to the appropriate companies. The process is quick and relatively uncomplicated.

****

8

Buying and Selling in Scotland

Scotland has it own system of law, and buying and selling a house or flat is quite a different process from doing so in England, Wales or Northern Ireland. The system generally works more quickly and there is less risk of gazumping.

Looking for property
Solicitors, property centres and offices. These are the largest source of properties available in Scotland. Often found in town centres, the property centres provide information in a similar way to estate agents outside Scotland.

Newspapers.
Daily Scottish newspapers are a good source of property. Regional and local newspapers carry many details on a regular basis.

Estate agents. These offer the same service

Ownership of property in Scotland
Property in Scotland does not exist as freehold or leasehold, as in England. Instead a "feudal tenure" system exists. This means that, as in freehold, the owner has right to building and land. However, the original owner of the development still has some say over any alterations and use of the land.

These feuing conditions are permanent and should be checked before purchase is considered. A new owner (feuar) can negotiate to have conditions waived, but there may be a charge for this. Further details of the system can be obtained from the lands tribunal for Scotland or your solicitor.

House prices

Property in Scotland is normally sold as "offers over" (sometimes called the upset price) the price set is usually the minimum and may not be negotiated down. This method is used where the property is likely to prove popular and to get the best price. If a quick sale is required a property may be sold as "fixed price" the seller will take the first offer at that price.

If there is more than one prospective purchaser the seller may opt to set a closing date for offers. The process is then like a blind bid, with none of the buyers knowing the price anyone else is bidding. Although the seller usually accepts the highest price, this is not always the case; other factors, such as date of entry, may be taken into consideration.

The buying process

Surveys

These are carried out before a formal offer is made. In some circumstances you may end up losing money, if your offer is not accepted. There are no licensed conveyancers in Scotland. Because solicitors do all the conveyancing and are so involved in the process then they will usually arrange surveys.

Making an offer

Your interest in buying a house is relayed via your solicitor to the selling solicitor by word of mouth. It does not have any legal standing and either party may pull out. Formal offer comes by letter, through the solicitor, and will include any items such as fixtures and fittings. The letter forms part of contract of sale.

Exchange of missives

If the offer is accepted, a formal letter called qualified acceptance is returned by the sellers solicitor, confirming or amending the conditions. The entry date may need to be negotiated to suit both parties. These formal letters are referred to as missives and may go back and forth for clarification.

Missives concluded

Once all the conditions are agreed, the purchase is then legally binding for both buyer and seller. The missives are concluded by the acting solicitors: neither the buyer or the seller signs anything. There is no deposit paid in the Scottish system except if you are buying a new house from a property developer

The law states that once the missives have been concluded, the purchaser is responsible for the insurance of the property. However, it is more usual for an agreement to be made in the missives that the seller remains liable until the date of entry.

The date that you would like to move is suggested in your formal offer to the seller. In this time you should be able to sell your house and complete any legal work. Before the date of entry, your solicitor will prepare what is known as a disposition to confirm the change of ownership. He will obtain from the sellers solicitor the title deeds which will be signed by the seller to agree the change of ownership. These will be handed over on the date of entry following payment of the property price.

Searches

There are two types of searches in Scotland:

Immediately prior to exchanging missives a search on the property and against the individual is made. This checks that the seller has a good title to the property and that the purchaser can grant security for the loan. In addition, a local authority search forms part of the missives. It checks that there are no proposed developments that would affect the property.

Selling a house or flat
Ways of selling your home

The majority of houses are bought and sold through solicitor offices, but you also have the options of selling through an estate agent or selling it privately yourself. Whatever option you choose, it is customary in Scotland to show prospective buyers around the house and explain the details.

DIY selling

This involves setting the price, preparing the sales details about the house, advertising it and showing people around. The advantages of this kind of sale are that you cut out middlemen and save commission. However, you will need a solicitor for conveyancing.

Selling through an estate agent

These are normally Scottish branches of well-known chains of agents. They offer a service similar to their English counterparts. In contrast to selling through a solicitor, estate agents often encourage you to take the first offer rather than generating interest and setting a closing date. You should get quotes from agents about their charges. this will be typically around 1.5% of selling price.

Selling through a solicitor

Most property in Scotland is sold through solicitors. They provide a service similar to estate agents and have property centres displaying details of houses for sale, although there may be an extra one off charge for this depending on the area you are in. Their commission charges are often slightly cheaper than those of estate agents. It is normal practice to use the same solicitor to sell your house and carry out the legal side of the sale.

The selling process

Your solicitor or estate agent will prepare the sales particulars and discuss the selling price with you as part of their contract. Depending upon the circumstances, they will advise as to whether the house is sold as "offers above" or as "fixed price". The former is usually set slightly below the expected price to encourage buyers. If a degree of competitiveness is created you may be able to set a "closing" date which usually achieves a better selling price.

Legally you should leave all fixtures and fittings, such as carpets and curtains or kitchen equipment unless you draw up a contract which states otherwise.

The legal services of your solicitor
There are two main areas the solicitor will need to follow up to allow smooth progress of a house sale.

The title deeds will need to be examined to check that you are the true owner of the property. Scottish law includes the Matrimonial Homes (Family Protection) (Scotland) Act: even if only one spouse owns the property permission to sell must be given by the partner.

Conveyancing will involve property surveys, and local searches to check there are no proposals for developments. If you are using a solicitor to sell your house, they may offer an overall charge that covers selling and legal services.

Accepting offers
Your solicitor will inform you if anyone has shown an interest in your property. If a lot of interest is shown in your house, you could consider setting a closing date for offers. Your solicitor or estate agent should advise you whether this is a good idea. There is no point in setting a date until you are sure more than one person is likely to make a formal offer.

The closing date is a specific time on a specific day that all formal offers will be assessed. You are not obliged to accept any offer if they are too low. Nor does the highest offer have to be accepted.

If you accept the highest offer, your solicitor may negotiate points concerning other conditions, such as extras included or dates, but there must be no attempt to try to raise the price offered. If you are using an estate agent, their role ends once the offer has been handed over to the solicitor.

A formal offer will include all the conditions of sale, the price, any items included, and the date of entry. Some offers are made with a time limit in which you must accept verbally, which can be as little as within 24 hours. You should seek advice from your solicitors whether to act promptly. You may be advised to hold out for a higher offer. If the purchaser is seriously interested they will not mind waiting for an acceptance.

Your solicitor will engage in the process of exchanging missives with the buyers solicitor. Missives are formal letters laying down conditions of sale and may be passed back and forth until an amicable agreement is reached. Once final missives have been exchanged the contract is legally binding for both parties, so it is important that you are familiar with all the conditions being negotiated by your solicitor through the missives. It will be too late once they have finally been changed.

Setting an entry date

The date for finalising the sale is suggested by both the seller and by the buyer in his offer. It is negotiated by both parties and a mutually agreed date is written into the missives. This is the date when the keys are handed to your solicitor, and you must move out. Although the date of entry is set by the seller, it may need to be changed to achieve a compromise which suits you and the purchaser.

Completion

Title deeds. Your buyer's solicitor will need to prepare the disposition and for this your solicitor will send the title deeds. The disposition is the document that states the change of ownership on the title deeds, and will need to be signed by you. It is handed over to the purchaser's solicitor in exchange for payment of the property on the date of settlement.

Now read the Key Points from Chapter Eight overleaf.

Key Points From Chapter 8

1   The process of buying and selling property in Scotland is quite different to that in England.

2   Property in Scotland does not exist as freehold or leasehold. Instead a Feudal tenure exists.

3   "Gazumping" is not possible in Scotland. Once an offer is made it is virtually binding.

4   Solicitors play a very important part in the process of buying and selling property in Scotland.

9

Buying Overseas

Thousands of Britons have purchased properties overseas. However, this can be problematic and certainly basic advice is needed relating to the particular country where you are buying. There are a few general tips when buying abroad:

- Buy through a qualified and licensed agent. In most countries including France, Spain, Portugal and the USA, agents legally have to be licensed and using an unlicensed agent means that there is no comeback if things go wrong.
- Do not sign anything until you are sure that you understand it. Note that estate agents in the above countries will tend to do more of the legal work than in Britain and hence charge more commission.
- Always hire a solicitor (English speaking if you are not fluent in the local language) to act for you. In some countries, the locals do not use solicitors but you should insist. The solicitor will check that the seller owns the property and that there are no debts attached to it and that planning regulations have been met. Local searches are not as regulated as they are in the UK and it's often a case of making informal enquiries at the local town hall.
- Understand the role played by the state notary (notaire in France, notario in Spain) he or she is a state official, whose only role is to see that the sale is completed. He or she will not act for you or the seller.

There are a number of useful websites where more information can be gained:
www.french-property-news.com
This site is the online arm of the magazine French Property News. It claims to have the most comprehensive list of properties on the web and also has

details of other organisations.

www.french-property.com

Similar to the above

www.europropertynet.com

This is a European wide estate agency service, carrying a wide range of properties from around Europe, including France, Spain, Portugal and Greece. Other advice is also available on this site.

For property in Spain, try www.spanishpropertyco.co.uk which specialises in retirement property.

For property in Eastern Europe you should go to www.eurobrix.com

Other useful websites:
For the USA-

www.primelocation.com

www.propertyshowrooms.com

www.escape2usa.co.uk

Property overseas generally
www.property-abroad.com

There are many other websites dealing with buying and selling property in most countries of the world. It goes without saying that you should learn as much about a country as possible and deal with professionals only before taking the plunge overseas.

10

Renting Out Your Property-Finding a Tenant

If you have decided to rent out your property, possibly because of difficulties in selling, it will be necessary to look at the possible sources of the tenant. The tenant is the key to your future income and profit and also to your own personal peace or otherwise and therefore must be chosen extremely carefully. You will need to decide what type of tenant you want, i.e. professional, working or whether you will accept DSS. Once you have an idea of the type of person you can then begin the process of looking.

Letting Agents
The government has announced (2014) that all lettings agents will in future have to join an Ombudsman scheme. This is in the light of the rising number of complaints which corresponds to the rising prominence of the private rented sector.

If you choose carefully, and choose an agent with a good track record, then there are obvious advantages in using an agent: they are likely to have tenants on their books: They are likely to be experienced and can vet tenants properly before signing a tenancy; they can provide you with a tenancy agreement and they can provide a service after the property is let. However, agents charge for this service and their fees can vary enormously. It is up to you as a would-be landlord to ensure you understand what it is they are charging and exactly what you are left with after the charges.

Some agencies will offer a guaranteed income for the duration of the contract that you have signed with them, even if a tenant leaves. However, you should be extremely careful as a number of cases recently against such agencies have revealed that there are unscrupulous operators around. If you do appoint an agent to manage a property you should agree at the outset, in writing, exactly what constitutes management. Failure to understand the deal between you and the agent can cost you dearly. For example, in a lot of cases, an agent will charge you a fixed fee, sometimes 1 months rental, for finding a tenant, but will then exercise the right that they have given themselves in the initial contract to sign a new agreement and charge another months rent after the tenancy has expired. In this way they will charge you a months rent every six months for doing nothing at all. Agents will typically look after the following:

1   Transfer the utility bills and the council tax into the name of the tenant. Sign agreements and take up references.
2   Paying for repairs, although an agent will only normally do this if rent is being paid directly to them and they can make appropriate deductions.
3   Chase rent arrears.
4   Serve notices of intent to seek possession if the landlord instructs them to do so. An agent cannot commence court proceedings except through a solicitor.
5   Visit the property at regular intervals and check that the tenants are not causing any damage.
6   Dealing with neighbour complaints.
7   Banking rental receipts if the landlord is abroad.
8   Dealing with housing benefit departments if necessary

Beware! There are many so-called rental agencies, which have sprang up since the property recession and also the advent of "Buy to Let". These agents are not professional, do not know a thing about property management, are shady and should be avoided like the plague. Shop around and seek a reputable agent. A typical management fee might be 10-15 percent of the rent, although there is lots of competition and lower prices can be obtained. As stated, there are many ways of charging and you should be clear about this. It is illegal for agencies to charge tenants for giving out a landlord's name and address. Most agencies will charge the landlord.

Advertisements

The classified advertisement section of local papers is a good place to seek potential tenants, particularly if you wish to avoid agency charges. Local papers are obviously cheaper than the nationals such as the Evening Standard in London or the broadsheets such as the Guardian. The type of newspaper you advertise in will largely reflect what type of customer you are looking for. An advert in the pages of the Times would indicate that you are looking for a well-heeled professional and this would be reflected in the type of property that you have to let.

There are many free ad papers and also you may want to go to student halls of residence or hospitals in order to attract a potential tenant.

When you do advertise, you should indicate clearly the type of property, in what area, what is required, i.e., male or female only, and the rent. You should try and avoid abbreviations as this causes confusion.

The public sector

One other source of income is the local authority or housing association. Quite often, your property will be taken off your hands under a five-year contract and you will receive a rental income paid direct for this period, with agreed increases. However, the local authority or housing association will demand a high standard before taking the property off your hands and quite often the rent achieved will be lower than a comparable market rent, in return for full management and secure income.

If you wish to try this avenue then you should contact your local authority or nearest large association.

Company lets

Where the tenant is a company rather than an individual, the tenancy agreement will be similar to an assured shorthold but will not be bound by the six-month rule (see chapter eight for details of assured shorthold tenancies). Company lets can be from any length of time, from a week to several years, or as long as you like.

The major difference between contracts and standard assured shorthold agreements is that the contract will be tailored to individual needs, and the agreement is bound by the provisions of contract law. Company tenancies are bound by the provisions of contract law and not by the Housing Acts. Note: if you are considering letting to a company you must use a letting agent or solicitor. Most companies will insist on it.

The advantages of a landlord letting to a company are:

- A company or embassy has no security of tenure and therefore cannot be a sitting tenant.
- A company cannot seek to reduce the rent by statutory interventions.
- Rental payments are often made quarterly or six monthly in advance.
- The financial status of a company is usually more secure than that of an individual.
- Company tenants often require long-term lets to accommodate staff relocating on contracts of between one and five years.

The main disadvantages of company lets are:

- A company tenancy can only be to a bona fide company or embassy, not to a private individual.
- A tenancy to a partnership would not count as a company let and may have some security of tenure.
- If the tenant is a foreign government, the diplomatic status of the occupant must be ascertained, as the courts cannot enforce breaches of contract with somebody who possesses diplomatic immunity.
- A tenancy to a foreign company not registered in the UK may prove time consuming and costly if it becomes necessary to pursue claims for unpaid rent or damage through foreign courts.

Finding a Tenant

Short-lets

Although company lets can be of any length, it is becoming increasingly popular for companies to rent flats from private landlords on short-lets. A short-let is any let of less than six months. But here, it is essential to check the rules with any borough concerned. Some boroughs will not allow lets for less than three months, as they do not want to encourage transient people in the neighborhood.

Generally speaking, short-lets are only applicable in large cities where there is a substantial shifting population. Business executives on temporary relocation, actors and others involved in television production or film work, contract workers and visiting academics are examples of people who might require a short-let.

From a landlord's point of view, short-lets are an excellent idea if you have to vacate your own home for seven or eight months, say, and do not want to leave it empty for that time. Short-let tenants provide useful extra income as well as keeping an eye on the place. Or if you are buying a new property and have not yet sold the old one, it can make good business sense to let it to a short-let tenant.

Short-let tenants are, usually, from a landlord's point of view, excellent blue-chip occupants. They are busy professionals, high earners, out all day and used to high standards. As the rent is paid by the company there is no worry for the landlord on this score either.

A major plus of short-lets is that they command between 20-50 percent more rent than the optimum market rent for that type of property. The one downside of short-lets is that no agency can guarantee permanent occupancy.

Student lets

Many letting agencies will not consider students and a lot of landlords similarly are not keen. There is the perception that students will not look after a home and tend to live a lifestyle guaranteed to increase the wear and tear on a property. However, if handled correctly, student lets can be profitable. Although students quite often want property for only eight or nine months, agencies that deal with students make them sign for a whole year. Rent is guaranteed by confirmation that the student is a genuine student with references from parents, who act as guarantors.

There can be a lot of money made from student lets. However, the tenancy will require more avid policing because of the nature of student lifestyle.

The DSS and housing benefit

Very few letting agencies or landlords will touch DSS or housing benefit tenants. However, as with student lets, there is another side of the coin.

Quite often it is essential for a tenant on HB to have a guarantor, usually a homeowner, before signing a tenancy. Then it is up to the machinations of the benefit system to ensure that the landlord receives rent. The rent is assessed by a benefit officer, with the rent usually estimated at market price. There are rent levels set for each are that the benefit officer will not go above. The 'bedroom tax' limits the amount of benefit a tenant will get relative to the number of bedrooms that they need.

A deposit is paid normally and rent is paid direct to the landlord, although with the introduction of Universal Credit (which is still being rolled out as I write) rent will go direct to the tenant, which can create problems for landlords. This will require the tenant's consent No other conditions should be accepted by a private landlord. Rent certainly should not be paid direct to the tenant.

Although tenants on HB have a bad name, due to stereotyping, there are many reasons why a person may be on benefit and if housing benefit tenancies are managed well, then this can be a useful source of tenant.

Holiday lets

Before the Housing Act 1988 became law, many landlords advertised their properties as holiday lets to bypass the then rules regarding security of tenure. Strictly speaking, a holiday let is a property let for no more than a month to any one tenant. If the same tenant renews for another month then the landlord is breaking the law. Nowadays, holiday lets must be just that; let for a genuine holiday.

If you have a flat or cottage that you wish to let for holiday purposes, whether or not you live in it yourself for part of the year, you are entering into a quite different agreement with the tenant.

Holiday lets are not covered by the Housing Act. The contract is finalised by exchange of letters with the tenant where they place a deposit and the owner confirms the booking. If the let is not for a genuine holiday you may have problems in evicting the tenant, as the whole point of a holiday let is that it is for no more than a fixed period of a month. Generally speaking, certain services must be provided for the let to be deemed a holiday let. Cleaning services and changes of bed linen are essential. The amount paid by the holiday-maker will usually include utilities but would exclude use of the telephone, fax machine etc. If you have a property that you think is suitable for holiday let or wish to invest in one, there are numerous companies who will put you on to their books. However, standards are high and there are a certain number of criteria to be met, such as safety checks, before they will consider taking you on. If possible, you should talk to someone with some experience of this type of let before entering into an agreement with an agency. The usual problems may arise, such as ensuring occupancy all year round and the maintenance of your property, which will be higher due to a high turnover.

Showing the property to the tenant
Once you have found a tenant, the next stage is to make arrangements for viewing the property. It is a good idea to make all appointments on the same day in order to avoid wasting time. If you decide on a likely tenant, it is wise to take up references yourself if you are not using an agency who will do this for you. This will normally be a previous landlord's reference and also a bank reference plus a personal reference. Only when these have been received and you have established that the person(s) is/are safe should you go ahead. Make sure that no keys have been handed over until the cheque has been cleared and you are in receipt of a month's rent and a month's deposit.

Deposits
Tenancy Deposit Protection Scheme

The Tenancy Deposit Protection Scheme was introduced to protect all deposits paid to landlords after 6th April 2007. After this date, landlords and/or agents must use a government authorised scheme to protect deposits. The need for such a scheme has arisen because of the historical problem with deposits and the abuse of deposits by landlords. The scheme works as follows:

Moving into a property

At the beginning of a new tenancy agreement, the tenant will pay a deposit to the landlord or agent as usual. Within 14 days the landlord is required to give 30 the tenant details of how the deposit is going to be protected including:

- the contact details of the tenancy deposit scheme
- the contact details of landlord or agent
- how to apply for the release of the deposit
- what to do if there is a dispute about the deposit

There are three tenancy deposit schemes that a landlord can opt for:

Tenancy Deposit Solutions Ltd
www.mydeposits.co.uk
info@mydeposits.co.uk
The Tenancy Deposit Scheme
www.tds.gb.com
0845 226 7837
The Deposit Protection Service
www.depositprotection.com
0870 707 1 707

The schemes above fall into two categories, insurance based schemes and custodial schemes.

Custodial Scheme
- The tenant pays the deposit to the landlord
- The landlord pays the deposit into the scheme
- Within 14 days of receiving the deposit, the landlord must give the tenant prescribed information
- A the end of the tenancy, if the landlord and tenant have agreed how much of the deposit is to be returned, they will tell the scheme which returns the deposit, divided in the way agreed by the parties.
- If there is a dispute, the scheme will hold the disputed amount until the dispute resolution service or courts decide what is fair
- The interest accrued by deposits in the scheme will be used to pay for the running of the scheme and any surplus will be used to offer interest to the tenant, or landlord if the tenant isn't entitled to it.

Insurance based schemes

- The tenant pays the deposit to the landlord
- The landlord retains the deposit and pays a premium to the insurer (this is the key difference between the two schemes)
- Within 14 days of receiving a deposit the landlord must give the tenant prescribed information.
- At the end of the tenancy if the landlord and tenant agree how the deposit is to be divided or otherwise then the landlord will return the amount agreed
- If there is a dispute, the landlord must hand over the disputed amount to the scheme for safekeeping until the dispute is resolved
- If for any reason the landlord fails to comply, the insurance arrangements will ensure the return of the deposit to the tenant if they are entitled to it.

If a landlord or agent hasn't protected a deposit with one of the above then the tenant can apply to the local county court for an order for the landlord either to protect the deposit or repay it.

Rental guarantees

The landlord is always advised to obtain a guarantor if there is any potential uncertainty as to payment of rent. One example is where the tenant is on benefits. The guarantor will be expected to assume responsibility for the rent if the tenant ceases to pay at any time during the term of the tenancy. There is a sample guarantee form in the appendix to this book.

Be strictly business like. You are letting property for a profit and the tenants are the key to that profit. A mistake at the outset can cost you dearly for a long time to come. See chapter 13 and 15 for further information concerning the start of the tenancy.

In chapter six we will look at what should be provided under a tenancy agreement and in chapter seven we will explore the legal framework governing residential lettings.

Rental guarantees
The landlord is always advised to obtain a guarantor if there is any potential uncertainty as to payment of rent. One example is where the tenant is on benefits. The guarantor will be expected to assume responsibility for the rent if the tenant ceases to pay at any time during the term of the tenancy. There is a sample guarantee form in the appendix to this book.

Be strictly business like. You are letting property for a profit and the tenants are the key to that profit. A mistake at the outset can cost you dearly for a long time to come. See chapter 13 and 15 for further information concerning the start of the tenancy.

Now read the main points from chapter Ten.

Finding a Tenant

Main points from chapter Ten

- The right choice of tenant is crucial as this is the key to the return on your investment.

- You should make sure that you have all the facts about a letting agents terms and conditions before you enter into an agreement.

- The classified advertisement section in the local paper is a good place to seek potential tenants, especially if you wish to manage the property yourself.

- The public sector offers a full management service but often offer a lower rent.

- There are other avenues to explore, such as company lets, short lets, holiday lets and so on. Make sure that you fully understand the various markets and what each entails before entering into an agreement.

- Make sure that, when you have found a tenant that you take up references and a deposit, and ensure that the tenant is fully aware of all relevant details.

- Make sure that the tenant's deposit is fully protected with one of the authorized schemes.

11

Items Provided Under a Tenancy

Furniture

A landlords decision whether or not to furnish property will depend on the sort of tenant that he is aiming to find. The actual legal distinction between a furnished property and an unfurnished property has faded into insignificance. If a landlord does let a property as furnished then the following would be the absolute minimum:

- Seating, such as a sofa and an armchair.
- Cabinet or sideboard.
- Kitchen tables and chairs.
- Cooker and refrigerator.
- Bedroom furniture.

Even unfurnished lets, however, are expected to come complete with a basic standard of furniture, particularly carpets and kitchen goods. If the landlord does supply electrical equipment then he or she will be responsible for carrying out annual checks along with annual checks on the boiler.

Services

Usually, a landlord will only provide services to a tenant if the property is a flat situated in a block or house split into flats or is a house on a private estate. The services will include cyclical painting and maintenance, usually on a three to four year basis (flats) and gardening and cleaning plus repairs to the communal areas, plus communal electricity bills and water rates. These services should be outlined in the agreement and administered within a strict framework of law. The 1985 Landlord and Tenant Act Section 18-30 as amended by the 1987 LTA and the 1996 Housing Act as amended by the 2002 Commonhold and Leasehold Reform Act are the main areas of law.

The landlord has rigid duties imposed within the Acts, such as the need to gain estimates before commencing works and also to consult with residents where the cost exceeds £250 per flat. The landlord must give the tenant 28 days notice of works to be carried out and a further 28 days to consider estimates, inviting feedback.

Tenants have the right to see audited accounts and invoices relating to work. Service charges, as an extra payment over and above the rent are always contentious and it is an area that landlords need to be aware of if they are to manage professionally.

Repairs
See chapter on repairs and improvements.

Insurance
Strictly speaking, there is no legal duty on either landlord or tenant to insure the property. However, it is highly advisable for the landlord to provide buildings insurance as he/she stands to lose a lot more in the event of fire or other disaster than the tenant. In addition, mortgagors will always want insurance in place to protect their own investment.

A landlord letting property for a first time would be well advised to consult his/her insurance company before letting as there are different criteria to observe when a property is let and not to inform the company could invalidate the policy.

At the end of the tenancy
The tenancy agreement will normally spell out the obligations of the

tenant at the end of the term. Essentially, the tenant will have an obligation to:

- Have kept the interior clean and tidy and in a good state of repair and decoration.
- Have not caused any damage.
- Have replaced anything that they have broken.
- Replace or pay for the repair of anything that they have damaged.
- Pay for the laundering of the linen.
- Pay for any other laundering.
- Put anything that they have moved or removed back to how it was.

Sometimes a tenancy agreement will include for the tenants paying for anything that is soiled at their own expense, although sensible wear and tear is allowed for. The landlord will normally be able to recover any loss from the deposit that the tenant has given on entering the premises (see previous chapter for details of the Deposit Protection Schemes). However, sometimes, the tenants will withhold rent for the last month in order to recoup their deposit. The introduction of the Deposit Protection Schemes have made this more difficult in practice. It is up to the landlord to negotiate reimbursement for any damage caused, but this should be within reason. There is a remedy, which can be pursued in the small claims court if the tenants refuse to pay but this is rarely successful.

Now read the main points from chapter Eleven.

Items Provided Under a Tenancy

Main points from Chapter Eleven

- A landlord's decision to furnish a property will depend on the sort of tenant he is aiming to find.

- Even unfurnished lets are expected to come complete with a basic standard of furniture.

- Usually, the landlord will only supply services to a tenant if the flat is in a block or a house on a private estate.

- If services are provided tenants have a right to audited accounts annually.

12

The Type of Tenancy to Use

The assured tenant

As a prospective landlord, even for the short term, you will need to know a little about the law relating to private lettings.

All tenancies, with the exceptions detailed, entered into after 15th January 1989, are known as assured tenancies. The *assured shorthold tenancy*, which is the most common form of tenancy used by the landlord nowadays, is one type of assured tenancy, and is for a fixed term of six months minimum and can be brought to an end with two months notice by serving a section 21 (of the Housing Act 1988) notice.

Assured tenancies are governed by the 1988 Housing Act, as amended by the 1996 Housing Act. It is to these Acts, or outlines of the Acts that the landlord must refer when intending to sign a tenancy and let a residential property. For a tenancy to be assured, three conditions must be fulfilled:

1. The premises must be a dwelling house. This basically means any premises, which can be lived in. Business premises will normally fall outside this interpretation.
2. There must exist a particular relationship between landlord and tenant. In other words there must exist a tenancy agreement. For example, a licence to occupy, as in the case of students, or accommodation occupied as a result of work, cannot be seen as a tenancy. Following on from this, the accommodation must be let as a single unit. The tenant, who must be an individual, must normally be able to sleep, cook and eat in the accommodation. Sharing of bathroom facilities will not prevent a tenancy being an assured tenancy but shared cooking or other facilities, such as a living room, will.

3. The third requirement for an assured tenancy is that the tenant must occupy the dwelling as his or her only or principal home. In situations involving joint tenants at least one of them must occupy.

Tenancies that are not assured
A tenancy agreement will not be assured if one of the following conditions applies:

- The tenancy or the contract was entered into before 15th January 1989.
- If no rent is payable or if only a low rent amounting to less than two thirds of the present ratable value of the property is payable.
- If the premises are let for business purposes or for mixed residential and business purposes.
- If part of the dwelling house is licensed for the sale of liquor for consumption on the premises. This does not include the publican who lets out a flat.
- If the dwelling house is let with more than two acres of agricultural land.
- If the dwelling house is part of an agricultural holding and is occupied in relation to carrying out work on the holding.
- If the premises are let by a specified institution to students, i.e., halls of residence.
- If the premises are let for the purpose of a holiday.
- Where there is a resident landlord, e.g., in the case where the landlord has let one of his rooms but continues to live in the house.
- If the landlord is the Crown (the monarchy) or a government department. Certain lettings by the Crown are capable of being assured, such as some lettings by the Crown Estate Commissioners.
- If the landlord is a local authority, a fully mutual housing association (this is where you have to be a shareholder to be a tenant) of a newly created Housing Action Trust or any similar body listed in the 1988 Housing Act.
- If the letting is transitional such as a tenancy continuing in its original

form until phased out, such as a protected tenancy under the 1977 Rent Act.

- Secure tenancy granted before 15th January 1989, e.g., from a local authority or housing association. These tenancies are governed by the 1985 Housing Act).

The Assured Shorthold tenancy

The assured shorthold tenancy is the most common form of tenancy used in the private sector. The main principle of the assured shorthold tenancy is that it is issued for a period of six months minimum and can be brought to an end by the landlord serving two months notice on the tenant. At the end of the six-month period the tenant, if given two months prior notice, by the landlord serving a section 21 notice (see appendix) must leave.

The section 21 notice, so called because it arises out of Section 21 of the 1988 Housing Act, is the pro-forma that all landlords must use when ending a tenancy.

If the notice is served on a tenant after the expiry of the initial six-month period it will be served as a s21 B notice which is for fixed-term periodic tenancies. It should be noted that the landlord must have complied with the provisions of the relevant tenancy deposit scheme and issued prescribed information to the tenant within 30 days of receipt of deposit otherwise the section 21 notice served at the outset of the tenancy will be invalid. Any property let on an assured tenancy can be let on an assured shorthold, providing the following conditions are met:

- The tenancy must be for a fixed term of not less than six months.
- The agreement cannot contain powers, which enable the landlord to end the tenancy before six months. This does not include the right of the landlord to enforce the grounds for possession, which will be approximately the same as those for the assured tenancy (see below).
- A notice requiring possession at the end of the term is usually served two months before that date.
- A notice must be served before any rent increase giving one month's clear notice and providing details of the rent increase.

Tenancy running on after fixed term

An assured shorthold tenancy will become periodic (will run from week to week) when the initial term of six months has elapsed and the landlord has not brought the tenancy to an end. If the tenancy runs on after the end of the fixed term then the landlord can regain possession by giving the required two months notice, as mentioned above. At the end of the term for which the assured shorthold tenancy has been granted, the landlord has an automatic right to possession.

Evicting assured shorthold tenants

As discussed, it is possible to gain possession of a property before the end of the fixed term if the tenancy has been seriously breached. Assured shorthold tenants, can be evicted only on certain grounds some discretionary, some mandatory (see below). i\n order for the landlord of an assured shorthold tenant to regain possession of the property, using grounds for possession such as non-payment of rent, a notice of seeking possession (of property) must be served, giving fourteen days notice of expiry and stating the ground for possession. Following the fourteen days a court order must be obtained. Although gaining a court order is not complicated, a solicitor will usually be used. Court costs can be awarded against the tenant.

Security of tenure: The ways in which a tenant can lose their home as an assured (shorthold) tenant

There are a number of circumstances called grounds (mandatory and discretionary) whereby a landlord can start a court action to evict a tenant. The following are the mandatory grounds (where the judge must give the landlord possession) and discretionary grounds (where the judge does not have to give the landlord possession) on which a court can order possession if the home is subject to an assured tenancy.

The mandatory grounds for possession

There are eight mandatory grounds for possession, which, if proved, leave the court with no choice but to make an order for possession.

- *Ground One* is used where the landlord has served a notice, no later than at the beginning of the tenancy, warning the tenant that this ground may be used against him/her.

  This ground is used where the landlord wishes to recover the property as his or her principal (first and only) home or the spouse's (wife's or husbands) principal home. The ground is not available to a person who bought the premises for gain (profit) whilst they were occupied.

- *Ground Two* is available where the property is subject to a mortgage and if the landlord does not pay the mortgage, could lose the home.

- *Grounds Three and Four* relate to holiday lettings.

- *Ground Five* is a special one, applicable to ministers of religion.

- *Ground Six* relates to the demolition or reconstruction of the property.
- *Ground Seven* applies if a tenant dies and in his will leaves the tenancy to someone else: but the landlord must start proceedings against the new tenant within a year of the death if he wants to evict the new tenant.

- *Ground Eight* concerns rent arrears. This ground applies if, both at the date of the serving of the notice seeking possession and at the date of the hearing of the action, the rent is at least 8 weeks in arrears or two months in arrears. This is the main ground used by landlords when rent is not being paid.

One of the advantages of a court order is that you will have details of the tenant's employers and can get an attachment of earnings against the tenant.

The discretionary grounds for possession of a property
As we have seen, the discretionary grounds for possession are those in

relation to which the court has some powers over whether or not the landlord can evict. In other words, the final decision is left to the judge. Often the judge will prefer to grant a suspended order first, unless the circumstances are dramatic.

- *Ground Nine* applies when suitable alternative accommodation is available or will be when the possession order takes effect. As we have seen, if the landlord wishes to obtain possession of his or her property in order to use it for other purposes then suitable alternative accommodation has to be provided.

- *Ground Ten* deals with rent arrears as does ground eleven. These grounds are distinct from the mandatory grounds, as there does not have to be a fixed arrear in terms of time scale, e.g., 8 weeks. The judge, therefore, has some choice as to whether or not to evict. In practice, this ground will not be relevant to managers of assured shorthold tenancies.

- *Ground Twelve* concerns any broken obligation of the tenancy. As we have seen with the protected tenancy, there are a number of conditions of the tenancy agreement, such as the requirement not to racially or sexually harass a neighbour. Ground Twelve will be used if these conditions are broken.

- *Ground Thirteen* deals with the deterioration of the dwelling as a result of a tenant's neglect. This is connected with the structure of the property and is the same as for a protected tenancy. It puts the responsibility on the tenant to look after the premises.

- *Ground Fourteen* concerns nuisance, annoyance and illegal or immoral use. This is where a tenant or anyone connected with the tenant has caused a nuisance to neighbours.

- *Ground Fourteen A* this ground deals with domestic violence.

- *Ground Fifteen* concerns the condition of the furniture and tenants neglect. As Ground thirteen puts some responsibility on the tenant to look after the structure of the building so Ground Fifteen makes the tenant responsible for the furniture and fittings.

The description of the grounds above is intended as a guide only. For a fuller description please refer to the 1988 Housing Act, section 7, Schedule two,) as amended by the 1996 Housing Act) which is available at reference libraries.

As we have discussed, it is usual for the landlord of an assured shorthold tenancy to serve a notice requiring possession on the tenant giving two months notice. It is unusual for a landlord to take an assured shorthold tenant to court on one of the grounds for possession. However, these circumstances do arise, where a tenant has breached the tenancy very early on and the landlord cannot wait for the fixed term to expire.

Fast track possession

In November 1993, following changes to the County Court Rules, a facility was introduced which enables landlords of tenants with assured shorthold tenancies to apply for possession of their property without the usual time delay involved in waiting for a court date and attendance at court. This is known as "fast track possession" It cannot be used for rent arrears or other grounds. It is used to gain possession of a property when the fixed term of six months or more has come to an end, a valid section 21 notice has been served and the tenant will not move.

Raising rent-How frequently can a landlord raise the rent?

The landlord should agree with the tenant the rent and arrangements for paying it before the tenancy begins. The details should be included in the tenancy agreement. If the tenancy is for a fixed term, the agreement should say either that the rent will be fixed for the length of the term or that it will be reviewed at regular intervals and how it will be reviewed. If the tenancy is a contractual periodic tenancy the tenancy agreement should say how often the rent will be reviewed and how it will be reviewed.

If the tenancy agreement does not say when the rent will increase, then if the tenancy is a fixed term the landlord can only put the rent up if the tenant agrees. If the tenant does not agree the landlord has to wait until the fixed term expires. If the tenancy is a contractual periodic tenancy, the landlord can put the rent up if the tenant agrees. Alternatively, the landlord can use a formal procedure in the 1988 Housing Act to propose a rent increase to be payable a year after the tenancy began.

When a fixed term tenancy ends and the tenancy lapses into a statutory periodic tenancy, the landlord can put the rent up if the tenant agrees.

Now read the main points from chapter Twelve

Main Points from Chapter Twelve

- **Assured tenancies**. All tenancies signed after 15th January 1989, with a few exceptions, are assured tenancies. The assured shorthold tenancy is one type of assured tenancy and is the one most frequently used by private landlords.

- **Protection**. Assured tenancies are not protected by the 1977 Rent Act and do not have a right to a fair rent.

- **Security**. Assured tenants can only be evicted on certain grounds for possession, after being given a minimum of fourteen days notice and taken to court.

- **Rents**. Assured rents cannot be raised more than once in a one-year period for the same tenant, unless the tenant agrees. They can, however, be raised when a fixed term assured shorthold has ended. This may be after six months.

- **Fixed term**. An assured shorthold tenancy is granted for a minimum period of six months. Two months notice has to be given before ending the tenancy. The notice can be served when granting the tenancy bringing it to an end on the last day of the six months. After the six months has elapsed, two months notice can be given anytime. The tenancy can be allowed to run on, it becomes an assured shorthold periodic tenancy, as opposed to fixed term.

13

Joint Tenancies

Joint tenancies: the position of two or more people who have a tenancy agreement for one property
Although it is the normal state of affairs for a tenancy agreement to be granted to one person, this is not always the case.

A tenancy can also be granted to two or more people and is then known as a joint tenancy. The position of joint tenants is exactly the same as that of single tenants. In other words, there is still one tenancy even though it is shared.

Usually people who are joint tenants are:

- Married couples
- Couples with a registered civil partnership
- Couples who cohabit
- Family members

Each tenant is responsible for paying the rent and observing the terms and conditions of the tenancy agreement. No one joint tenant can prevent another joint tenant's access to the premises.

If one of the joint tenants dies then his or her interest will automatically pass to the remaining joint tenants. A joint tenant cannot dispose of his or her interest in a will.

If one joint tenant, however, serves a notice to quit (notice to leave the property) on another joint tenant(s) then the tenancy will come to an end and the landlord can apply to court for a possession order, if the remaining tenant does not leave.

The position of a wife or husband in relation to joint tenancies is rather more complex because the married person has more rights when it comes to the home than the single person.

Remember, the position of a tenant who has signed a joint tenancy agreement is exactly the same as that of the single tenant. If one person leaves, the other(s) have the responsibilities of the tenancy. If one person leaves without paying his share of the rent then the other tenants will have to pay instead.

Now read the Main Points from Chapter Thirteen

Main points from Chapter Thirteen

- **Joint tenants**. A tenancy granted to two or more people is a joint tenancy. The position of joint tenants is exactly the same as that of a single tenant.

- **Ending the tenancy**. In order to end the tenancy, one of the joint tenants must serve a notice to quit on the other tenant(s).

14

Carrying Out Repairs and Improvements

Repairs and improvements generally: The landlord and tenants obligations

Repairs are essential works to keep the property in good order. Improvements and alterations to the property, e.g. the installation of a shower.

As we have seen, most tenancies are periodic, i.e. week-to-week or month-to-month. If a tenancy falls into this category, or is a fixed-term tenancy for less than seven years, and began after October 1961, then a landlord is legally responsible for most major repairs to the flat or house.

If a tenancy began after 15th January 1989 then, in addition to the above responsibility, the landlord is also responsible for repairs to common parts and service fittings.

The area of law dealing with the landlord and tenants repairing obligations is the 1985 Landlord and Tenant Act, section 11.

This section of the Act is known as a covenant and cannot be excluded by informal agreement between landlord and tenant. In other words the landlord is legally responsible whether he or she likes it or not. Parties to a tenancy, however, may make an application to a court mutually to vary or exclude this section.

Example of repairs a landlord is responsible for:
- Leaking roofs and guttering.
- Rotting windows.
- Rising damp.
- Damp walls.

- Faulty electrical wiring.
- Dangerous ceilings and staircases.
- Faulty gas and water pipes.
- Broken water heaters and boilers.
- Broken lavatories, sinks or baths.

In shared housing the landlord must see that shared halls, stairways, kitchens and bathrooms are maintained and kept clean and lit.

Normally, tenants are responsible only for minor repairs, e.g., broken door handles, cupboard doors, etc. Tenants will also be responsible for decorations unless they have been damaged as a result of the landlord's failure to do repair.

A landlord will be responsible for repairs only if the repair has been reported. It is therefore important to report repairs in writing and keep a copy. If the repair is not carried out then action can be taken. Damages can also be claimed.

Compensation can be claimed, with the appropriate amount being the reduction in the value of the premises to the tenant caused by the landlord's failure to repair. If the tenant carries out the repairs then the amount expended will represent the decrease in value.

The tenant does not have the right to withhold rent because of a breach of repairing covenant by the landlord. However, depending on the repair, the landlord will not have a very strong case in court if rent is withheld.

Reporting repairs to landlords
The tenant has to tell the landlord or the person collecting the rent straight away when a repair needs doing. It is advisable that it is in writing, listing the repairs that need to be done.

Once a tenant has reported a repair the landlord must do it within a reasonable period of time. What is reasonable will depend on the nature of the repair. If certain emergency work needs to be done by the council, such as leaking guttering or drains a notice can be served ordering the landlord to do the work within a short time. In exceptional cases if a home cannot be made habitable at reasonable cost the council may declare that the house must no longer be used, in which case the council has a legal duty to re-house a tenant.

If after the council has served notice the landlord still does not do the work, the council can send in its own builder or, in some cases take the landlord to court. A tenant must allow a landlord access to do repairs. The landlord has to give twenty-four hours notice of wishing to gain access.

The tenants rights whilst repairs are being carried out
The landlord must ensure that the repairs are done in an orderly and efficient way with minimum inconvenience to the tenant If the works are disruptive or if property or decorations are damaged the tenant can apply to the court for compensation or, if necessary, for an order to make the landlord behave reasonably.

If the landlord genuinely needs the house empty to do the work he/she can ask the tenant to vacate it and can if necessary get a court order against the tenant.

A written agreement should be drawn up making it clear that the tenant can move back in when the repairs are completed and stating what the arrangements for fuel charges and rent are.

Can the landlord put the rent up after doing repairs?
If there is a service charge for maintenance, the landlord may be able to pass on the cost of the work(s).

Tenants rights to make improvements to a property
Unlike carrying out repairs the tenant will not normally have the right to insist that the landlord make actual alterations to the home. However, a tenant needs the following amenities and the law states that you should have:
- Bath or shower.
- Wash hand basin.
- Hot and cold water at each bath, basin or shower.
- An indoor toilet.

If these amenities do not exist then the tenant can contact the council's Environmental Health Officer. An improvement notice can be served on the landlord ordering him to put the amenity in.

Disabled tenants

If a tenant is disabled he/she may need special items of equipment in the accommodation. The local authority may help in providing and, occasionally, paying for these. The tenant will need to obtain the permission of the landlord. If you require more information then contact the social services department locally.

Shared housing. The position of tenants in shared houses (Houses in Multiple Occupation)

A major change to improve standards of shared housing was introduced in 2006. The parts of the Housing Act 2004 relating to the licensing of HMO's (Houses in Multiple Occupation) and the new Health and Safety Rating System for assessing property conditions came into effect on 6rh April 2006.

The Act requires landlords of many HMO's to apply for licences. The HMO's that need to be licensed are those with:

- Three or more storeys, which are
- Occupied by five or more people forming two or more households (i.e. people not related, living together as a couple etc) and
- Which have an element of shared facilities (eg kitchen, bathroom etc)

As far as licensing is concerned, attics and basements are included as storeys if they are used as living accommodation. Previously, HMO's were only defined as houses converted into flats or bedsits, but the new Act widens this definition and many more types of shared houses are now included.

A local authority will have a list of designated properties will have a list of those properties which are designated HMO's and they will need to be licensed.

Usually, landlords will need to apply to a local authority private sector unit for licences. It has been illegal for landlords to manage designated properties without a licence since July 2006.

Landlords will have to complete an application form and pay a fee, the local authority will then assess whether the property is suitable for the number of people the landlord wants to rent it to. In most case, the local authority, their agents, will visit a property to assess facilities and also fire precautions. A decision will then be taken to grant a license.

There is a fee for registration, councils set the fee and the ones shown below are indicative of a southern local authority:

- Shared houses-five sharers landlords first house £640
- Subsequent house £590
- Plus £10 each additional occupier over five

Hostels
- 10 occupiers £690
- 20 occupiers £790
- 50 occupiers £1100
- 75 occupiers £1340

In summary, The landlord of a HMO has certain duties under the regulations to his tenants:

Duty to provide information
The manager (this means that whoever is charged with the management of the building) must ensure that:

- His name, address and telephone number are available to each household in the HMO
- These details are also clearly displayed in a prominent position in the HMO.
-

The manager should maintain a log book to record all events at the property such as:

- Testing of fire alarms
- Testing of fire fighting equipment
- Gas safety certificate
- Electrical report
- Inspection and wants of repair

Duty to take safety measures

The manager must ensure that all means of escape from fire in the property are kept free from obstruction and in good order as should all fire alarms and equipment.

The manager should ensure that the structure is designed and maintained in a safe condition, and also take steps to protect occupiers from injury. In properties with four or more occupants, the Regulations provide that fire escape notices be clearly displayed.

Duty to maintain water supply drainage

The manager must ensure that the water supply and drainage system serving the property are maintained in a good working condition. More specifically, water fittings should be protected from frost and all water storage tanks should be provided with covers.

Duty to supply and maintain gas and electricity

The manager must supply the local housing authority within 7 days of receiving a written request a safety certificate. The manager must ensure that the fixed electrical installation is checked at least once every three years by a suitably qualified electrician and supply this to the LHA on written request.

In addition to the above, there is a duty to maintain common parts, fixtures, fittings and appliances. There is a duty to maintain living accommodation and to provide waste disposal facilities.

Powers of the local authority in relation to HMO's

It is essential to ensure that, if you have invested in a HMO that you manage it rigorously because local authorities have sweeping powers to fine landlords and to revoke licenses. A local authority can prosecute a landlord who does not obtain a license for a HMO.

Safety generally for all landlords

The main product safety regulations relevant to the lettings industry are:

Gas safety

The Gas safety (Installation and use) Regulations 1998
The Gas Cooking Appliances (safety) Regulations 1989
Heating Appliances(Fireguard) (safety) Regulations 1991
Gas Appliances(Safety) Regulations 1995

All of the above are based on the fact that the supply of gas and the appliances in a dwelling are safe. A Gas Safety certificate is required to validate this.

Furniture Safety

Furniture and Furnishings (Fire) (Safety) Regulations 1988 and 1993 (as amended)

Landlords and lettings agents are included in these regulations. The regulations set high standards for fire resistance for domestic upholstered furniture and other products containing upholstery. The main provisions are:

- Upholstered articles (i.e. beds, sofas, armchairs etc) must have fire resistant filling material.
- Upholstered articles must have passed a match resistant test or, if of certain kinds (such as cotton or silk) be used with a fire resistant interliner.
- The combination of the cover fabric and the filling material must have passed a cigarette resistance test.

The landlord should inspect property for non-compliant items before letting and replace with compliant items.

Electrical Safety

Electrical Equipment (Safety) Regulations 1994

Plugs and Sockets etc. (Safety) Regulations 1994.

The Electrical Equipment Regulations came into force in January 1995. Both sets of regulations relate to the supply of electrical equipment designed with a working voltage of between 50 and 1000 volts a.c. (or between 75 and 1000 volts d.c.) the regulations cover all the mains voltage household electrical goods including cookers, kettles, toasters, electric blankets, washing machines, immersion heaters etc. The regulations do not apply to items attached to land. This is generally considered to exclude the fixed wiring and built in appliances (e.g. central heating systems) from the regulations.

Lettings agents and landlords should take the following action:

Essential:

Check all electrical appliances in all managed properties on a regular fixed term basis. Remove unsafe items and keep a record of checks.

Recommended:

- Have appliances checked by a qualified electrical engineer
- Avoid purchasing second hand electrical items
- There is no specific requirement for regular testing under the regulations. However, it is recommended that a schedule of checks, say on an annual basis, is put in place.

The availability of grants

Disabled Facilities Grant

The only mandatory grant is the Disabled Facilities Grant, given to those in need, which has been assessed by an Occupational Therapist-the grant has a ceiling. Information of which can be obtained from the local authority. As the name suggests it is for those who are disabled and are n need of works which will make the property accessible and usable for disabled people.

Disabled Facilities Assistance
Disabled Facilities Assistance is in the form of interest free loans, repayable on disposal of the property. To qualify for DFA a person must be at least 18 years old and a freeholder or leaseholder with at least 10 years to expiry of lease and authority to do the work. The maximum amount of assistance is £25,000 or 50% of the equity existing at the time of application. There are a number of other conditions related to the actual works. Details can be obtained from the local authority.

There are a number of other grants available from local authorities and also central government. For details check with your local authority.

Sanitation health and hygiene

Local authorities have a duty to serve an owner with a notice requiring the provision of a WC when a property has insufficient sanitation, sanitation meaning toilet waste disposal.

They will also serve notice if it is thought that the existing sanitation is inadequate and is harmful to health or is a nuisance.

Local authorities have similar powers under various Public Health Acts to require owners to put right bad drains and sewers, also food storage facilities and vermin, plus the containing of disease.

The Environmental Health Department, if it considers the problem bad enough will serve a notice requiring the landlord to put the defect right. In certain cases the local authority can actually do the work and require the landlord to pay for it. This is called work in default.

Now read the main points from Chapter Fourteen overleaf.

Main points from chapter Fourteen

- **The law**. The landlord has repairing obligations under the Landlord and Tenant Act 1985, section 11.
- **Tenants responsibility**. Normally, tenants are responsible only for minor internal repairs.
- **Landlords responsibility**. A landlord will only be responsible for a repair if it has been reported.
- **Local authority**. If a landlord does not carry out repairs then the local authority in particular the Environmental Health Department can get involved.
- **Inconvenience**. A tenant has certain rights whilst repairs are being done, particularly for inconvenience.
- **Improvements**. A tenant will not normally have the right to make improvements. However, they are entitled to certain basic amenities, such as a shower or a bath.
- **Disabled**. A disabled tenant may need certain items of equipment in their home. The local authority can advise and assist in this area, even helping with payment.
- **Shared housing**. There are special laws governing housing in multiple occupation (shared housing) particularly in relation to health and safety. The local authority can advise.
- **Local authority grants.** Private tenants may be entitled to a grant to help with work on a property. The local authority will advise on entitlement.

15

Regaining Possession of a Property

Fast-track possession

In normal circumstances, the landlord will have served a section 21 notice on the tenant at the start of the tenancy. This brings the tenancy to an end on the day of expiry, i.e. on the day of expiry of the six month period, or 12 month period, whichever is appropriate. It should be noted that if a landlord takes a deposit from the tenant then every deposit must be registered with the appropriate deposit service before the landlord can serve the s21 notice. It should also be noted that if a section 21 notice is served after the end of the fixed term giving two months notice then the notice should be a section 21 (b). This is important as a service of the incorrect notice can delay proceedings.

On expiry of the notice, if it is the landlord's intention to take possession of the property then the tenants should leave. It is worthwhile writing a letter to the tenants one month before expiry reminding them that they should leave.

In the event of the tenant refusing to leave, then the landlord has to then follow a process termed 'fast track possession'. This entails filling in the appropriate forms (N5B) which can be downloaded from Her Majesty's Court Service Website www.justice.gov.uk.

Assuming that a valid section 21 notice has been served on the tenant, the accelerated possession proceedings can begin and the forms completed and lodged with the court dealing with the area where the property is situated. In order to grant the accelerated possession order the court will require the following:

- The assured shorthold agreement
- The section 21 notice
- Evidence of service of the section 21 notice

The best form of service of the s21 notice is by hand. If you have already served the notice then evidence that the tenant has received it will be required.

Having the correct original paperwork is of the utmost importance. Without this, the application will fail and delays will be incurred.

If the tenant disputes the possession proceedings in any way they will have 14 days to reply to the court. If the case is well founded and the paperwork is in order then there should be no case for defence. Once the accelerated possession order has been granted then this will need to be served on the tenant, giving them 14 days to vacate. In certain circumstances, if the tenant pleads hardship the court can grant extra time to leave, six weeks as opposed to two weeks. If they still do not vacate then an application will need to be made to court for a bailiffs warrant to evict the tenants.

Accelerated possession proceedings cannot be used against the tenant for rent arrears. It will be necessary to follow the procedure below.

An accelerated possession order remains in force for six years from the date it was granted.

Going to court to end the tenancy

There may come a time when you need to go to court to regain possession of your property. This will usually arise when the contract has been breached by the tenant, for non-payment of rent or for some other breach such as nuisance or harassment. As we have seen, a tenancy can be brought to an end in a court on one of the grounds for possession. However, as the tenancy will usually be an assured shorthold then it is necessary to consider whether you are in a position to give two months notice and withhold the deposit, as opposed to going to court. The act of withholding the deposit will entail you refusing to authorize the payment to the tenant online. This then brings arbitration into the frame. Deposit schemes have an arbitration system as an integral part of the scheme.

If you decide, for whatever reason, to go to court, then any move to regain your property for breach of agreement will commence in the county court in the area in which the property is. The first steps in ending the tenancy will necessitate the serving of a notice of seeking possession using one of the Grounds for Possession detailed earlier in the book. If the tenancy is protected then 28 days must be given, the notice must be in prescribed form and served on the tenant personally (preferably).

If the tenancy is an assured shorthold, which is more often the case now, then 14 days notice of seeking possession can be used. In all cases the ground to be relied upon must be clearly outlined in the notice. If the case is more complex, then this will entail a particulars of claim being prepared, usually by a solicitor, as opposed to a standard possession form.

A fee is paid when sending the particulars to court, which should be checked with the local county court. The standard form which the landlord uses for routine rent arrears cases is called the N119 and the accompanying summons is called the N5. Both of these forms can be obtained from the court or from www.courtservice.gov. When completed, the forms should be sent in duplicate to the county court and a copy retained for you.

The court will send a copy of the particulars of claim and the summons to the tenant. They will send you a form which gives you a case number and court date to appear, known as the return date.

On the return date, you should arrive at court at least 15 minutes early. You can represent yourself in simple cases but are advised to use a solicitor for more contentious cases.

When it is your turn to present the case, you should have your file in order, a copy of all relevant notices served and a current rent arrears figure or a copy of the particulars for other cases. If it is simple rent arrears then quite often the judge will guide you through. However, the following are the steps to observe:

• State your name and address.
• Tenants name and address.
• Start date of tenancy.
• Current rent and arrears.
• Date notice served-a copy should be produced for the judge.
• Circumstances of tenant (financial and other) this is where

you make your case.
•Copy of order wanted.

If the tenant is present then they will have a chance to defend themselves.

A number of orders are available. However, if you have gone to court on the mandatory ground eight then if the fact is proved then you will get possession immediately. If not, then the judge can grant an order, suspended whilst the tenant finds time to pay.

In a lot of cases, it is more expedient for a landlord to serve notice-requiring possession, if the tenancy has reached the end of the period, and then wait two months before the property is regained. This saves the cost and time of going to court particularly if the ground is one of nuisance or other, which will involve solicitors.

In many cases, if you are contemplating going to court and have never been before and do not know the procedure then it is best to use a solicitor to guide the case through. Costs can be recovered from the tenant, although this depends on the tenant's means.

If you regain possession of your property midway through the contractual term then you will have to complete the possession process by use of bailiff, pay a fee and fill in another form, Warrant for Possession of Land.

If you have reached the end of the contractual term and wish to recover your property then a fast track procedure is available which entails gaining an order for possession and bailiff's order by post. This can be used in cases with the exception of rent arrears.

Now read the main points from chapter fifteen.

Main points from Chapter Fifteen

- One of the unpleasant sides of being a landlord is that you may have to go to court to regain possession of a property.

- Any move to regain possession of your property will commence in the local county court where the property is. Fourteen days service of notice is needed and a fee is payable to the court. It is usually best to employ a solicitor to take this action.

- In many cases it is better to serve a section 21 notice and regain possession after two months rather than incur the expense of court action.

16

At the End of a Tenancy

When does the tenancy end?
The tenancy will end in one of the following situations:

1. At the end of the term when the tenant leaves voluntarily
2. When the tenant vacates after service of notice to terminate (served either by landlord or tenant)
3. By agreement with the landlord
4. When an order for possession has been made by the court.

Normally, the tenant leaves voluntarily, or surrenders the tenancy. A tenant cannot force the landlord to accept a surrender before the end of the term. If the tenant leaves mid way through the term the landlord can still claim rent from him to the end of the tenancy. You will not be able to collect rent from him when you re-let the property, except for rent arrears.

Sometimes a tenant will simply abandon the property before the tenancy is ended. However, the landlord has to be on very safe ground if he is wanting to repossess the property and re-let it. The landlord should check that all the possessions have gone and also check to see that the utilities have been cut off.

The bottom line is that if the landlord takes back the property and the tenant can prove that he has not vacated then the landlord is liable for damages.

Handover procedure
When it is time for the tenant to go, you should arrange for an

appointment with him at the property. The contents and condition of the property should be checked using the inventory and schedule of condition. You will then be able to decide how much, if any, of the deposit to retain. When making any retentions from the deposit you should allow for any fair wear and tear. If it is left in a dirty condition you are entitled to retain the reasonable costs of cleaning the property.

Tenants property left behind
This always poses a problem for landlords, because they will want to clear the property and re-let it as soon as possible. However, landlords need to be very careful when clearing goods that have been left behind, particularly when a property has been abandoned, as sometimes tenants can bring a claim for disposal of goods, even though they have abandoned.

The procedure for dealing with this situation is laid down in an Act called the Torts (Interference with Goods Act 1977 (not applicable in Scotland). Under this Act, the landlord can dispose of goods left behind as follows:

1. If the landlord sends a letter by recorded delivery to the tenant stating that he intends to sell/dispose of the goods and gives the following information:
• The name and address of the landlord (i.e. where he can be contacted about the items held)
• The place where they are held
• The date after which he intends to sell the goods (this must give the tenant a reasonable time to collect the goods –say two to four weeks)

Make sure you keep a copy of the letter sent. If the landlord doesn't have any address for the tenant, he can sell or dispose of the goods if he is able to show that he has made reasonable steps to contact him. Always have an independent witness when itemizing the goods.

If any of the goods are sold, the proceedings of sale are, strictly speaking, the tenants and should be kept for him. However, the landlord will be able to deduct the costs of sale and if there are rent arrears then these can be deducted too.

Death of a tenant

What happens if a tenant dies? If he is a joint tenant then the tenancy will devolve onto the other remaining tenant. If the tenant is a sole tenant then the tenants executors will usually contact the landlord to discuss the tenancy. In an assured shorthold tenancy there will be no right of succession as this will be contained within the mandatory grounds for possession.

For more advice on what to do when a tenant dies, guidance can be obtained from the Official Solicitor at www.officialsolicitor.gov.uk

17

Managing the Finances-Tax and Other Issues

This chapter explains some of the issues concerning allowances and taxation related to property that is being let out. It doesn't go into great depth, you would need an accountant to advise you on more complex matters, particularly if you are a landlord of multiple properties.

Allowable expenses

If you let out property you can deduct certain expenses and tax allowances from your rental income to work out your taxable profit and loss. If you have several UK residential lettings you pool the income and expenses together. Furnished holiday lettings and overseas lettings are worked out separately.

The expenses you can deduct from letting income (unless its under the rent a room scheme) include:

- Lettings agent's fees
- Legal fees for lettings of a year or less, or for renewing a lease for less than 50 years
- Accountants fees
- Buildings and contents insurance
- Interest on property loans
- Maintenance and repairs to the property (but not improvements
- Utility bills such as gas, electricity and water
- Rent, ground rent, service charges
- Council tax
- Services you pay for, such as cleaning and gardening

- Other direct costs of letting the property, such as phone calls, stationary and advertising

If your annual income for letting is less than £70,000 (before expenses) you include the total expenses on your tax return. If it is over £70,000 you need to provide a breakdown.

You can only claim expenses that are solely for running your property letting business. If the expense is only partly for running your business, or you live in the property yourself, then you may only be able to claim part of it.

Non-allowable expenses
When you work out profit, you can't deduct:

- 'Capital' costs, such as furniture or the property itself
- Personal expenses-costs that aren't to do with your lettings business
- Any loss you make when you sell the property

However, you may be able to claim some allowances instead. You should consult your accountant, or HMRC for further information about these allowances.

Furnished residential lettings
 For furniture and equipment provided with a furnished residential letting (excluding furnished holiday lettings) you can claim a wear and tear allowance. The allowance is 10% of the net rent-that is rent received less any costs that you pay that a tenant would normally pay, for example council tax.

As an alternative to the wear and tear allowance, you can claim a 'renewals allowance'. This allowance covers the cost of replacing furniture or equipment including small items like cutlery. To work it out, take the cost of the replacement item and deduct from it:

- The amount you sold the old one for (if anything)

- Anything extra you paid for a better one

Once you have chosen which of these allowances to claim for a property, you can't switch between them from year to year. You cannot claim capital allowances for equipment that is used in a dwelling house. Most residential accommodation is classed as a dwelling house.

Furnished holiday lettings
If you own a qualifying furnished holiday let in the UK, or European Union, you can claim capital allowances based on the cost of the furniture and equipment you provide with the property. Or you can claim a renewals allowance. You cannot claim wear and tear. See capital allowances below. Also, see section on furnished holiday lettings below.

All letting properties
You cannot claim capital allowances for furniture and fixtures for use in a dwelling house if you have a property rental business unless it qualifies as a furnished holiday lettings business. Whatever letting it is, you can claim a capital allowance on the cost of things that you need for running your property letting business, such as a computer. You can also claim for equipment that isn't for the use of a single let property, like a new fire alarm system for a block of flats.

How much capital allowance can you claim?
There are different types of allowances. In some cases you can claim the full cost of an item as a deduction in the year that you buy it. In other cases you can claim all of your expenditure on various items in the year that you buy them. You may have to work out the allowance as the percentage of the value in a pool of expenditure. The allowance is deducted along with other allowances in calculating your profit.

If you use an item for anything other than your business you will have to work out the allowance for that item separately. You can only claim the amount that is for business use.

Which year do expenses apply to?

You have to allocate expenses to the year that they apply to-it doesn't matter when you actually pay for them. However, for capital allowance purposes, it does matter when the cost of the item is payable. You may have to allocate part of the expense to one year and part to another.

Losses

If your lettings business makes a loss, you can carry it forward` to a later year and offset it against future profits from the same business. The rules for holiday lettings are slightly different and you should check with HMRC for further clarification.

Working out tax payable

Work out 'net profit' as follows:

- Add up all of your rental income
- Add up all of you allowable expenses
- Take allowable expenses away from income

If you have more than one residential letting, group all the income and expenses together.

To arrive at your taxable profit, deduct any allowable expenses away from your net profit. If you let furnished property, you can deduct either of the following:

- A wear and tear allowance-based on a percentage of your rent, as mentioned above
- A renewals allowance, as mentioned above

As stated, you can't claim both allowances.

Reporting profits to HMRC

If your profit is less than £2,500 and you are employed or paying tax on a pension then your tax code can be adjusted to collect tax on your property income each year.

If your profit is £2,500 or more or you are not on PAYE
In this case you will need to fill in a self- assessment tax return. If your total income from property is more than £70,000 in one tax year (based on 2014-2015) you must declare it on your tax return. You must also show your expenses separately. If it's below £70,000 you can group it as a single total on your return. When you fill in your return put the rent and expenses in the year that they relate to-it doesn't matter when you receive them.

How much tax is paid?
Your taxable profit form property letting is added to your income. Tax will be charged at the appropriate rate.

If you let property jointly, with someone else, when you fill in your tax returns you should each show your respective shares.

Capital gains tax
When you come to sell the property, you will be liable for CGT, but only on the gains that you have made. You have a personal CGT allowance of £11,000 a year (2014-2015). If the property is held in joint names, with a spouse or partner you can add your allowances together.

Any net taxable gain in the year is added to your total income from other sources in the year to determine the tax band applicable.

If the property was formerly your main residence, you are exempt from CGT if you sell within three years of it becoming a rental property. Where a gain is made on disposal of a property that has been a main residence at some point, but has also been specifically let as residential accommodation, then a further special relief is available. This exempts a gain of up to £40,000.

If the property was never your main residence, you are liable for full CGT for the first three years. After that, the proportion of the tax charged is tapered for the next seven years. There is a reduction of 5% each year after three years increasing by 5% each year to a maximum of 40% of the gain, after 10 years. This equates to effective tax rates for higher rate payers of 24% and 13.8% for lower rate payers.

Tax on furnished holiday lettings
If you let out a furnished holiday home in the UK or European Economic Area (EEA) you may be entitled to certain tax advantages. However, your property must meet some rules to qualify.

Rules for furnished holiday lettings for 2014-2015 tax year
To make sure that a property qualifies as a holiday letting, it must be:

- In the UK or EEA
- Furnished
- Available for commercial letting to the public, as holiday accommodation, for at least 210 days a year
- Commercially let as holiday accommodation for at least 105 days a year-the rent must be charged at market rent and not at cheap rates to friends or family
- A short term letting of no more than 31 days

Tax advantage of furnished holiday lettings
The tax advantages if your property qualifies as a holiday home are:
- You can claim capital allowances
- You get the benefit of some favorable capital gains tax rules when you sell, or otherwise dispose of the property.

Working out taxable profit
The profit on furnished holiday lettings is worked out in the same way as other lettings income. The only difference is that you can claim capital allowances rather than wear and tear allowances that other rental businesses receive. Examples of expenses that qualify for capital allowances include the cost of furnishings and furniture and equipment such as refrigerators and washing machines.

If you make a loss
You can carry a loss forward and offset it against future lettings profits. If you have a UK holiday home the losses can only reduce the future holiday

let profits of the UK home, likewise with a EEA holiday home. You cannot use a holiday let loss to reduce your other income.

If you sell or 'otherwise dispose' of the property

You may be able to take advantages of capital gains tax reliefs, such as 'business asset roll-over relief'. For example, if you reinvest the sale proceeds within three years in certain other business assets, you may be able to defer payment of Capital Gains Tax until you dispose of those new assets. More information can be obtained from HMRC.

You should declare your income from furnished holiday lets on your UK self-assessment tax return.

Keeping records

For all property lettings it is very important to keep records of all income and expenditure and associated receipts. As with all business, accurate record keeping is vital. As a guide, your records should include:

- All the rent you should receive and dates when you let out your property
- Any income from services provided to tenants
- Your business expenses
- Rent books, receipt, invoices and bank statements

Now read the main points from Chapter 17

Managing the Finances-Tax and Other Issues

Main points from Chapter Seventeen

- Anyone investing in property is liable to pay income tax

- There are two main categories of people who invest in property-the investor and the trader

- Relevant interest charges can be set off against income

- Renewals and wear and tear can be offset

- Certain maintenance costs-disregarding improvements can be offset against income

- Other charges such as rents, rates and insurance can be offset

- Capital gains tax is payable although can be minimized subject to HMRC rules

18

Private Tenancies in Scotland

The law governing the relationship between private landlords and tenants in Scotland is different to that in England. Since the beginning of 1989, new private sector tenancies in Scotland have been covered by the Housing (Scotland) Act 1988. Following the passage of this Act, private sector tenants no longer have any protection as far as rent levels are concerned and tenants enjoy less security of tenure.

There are four essential elements in the creation of a tenancy under Scottish law:

- An agreement between landlord and tenant.
- The payment of rent. If someone is allowed to occupy a property without an agreement then this will not amount to a tenancy.
- A fixed permission date (called an 'ish').
- Possession.

The agreement must be in writing if the tenancy is for a period of 1 year or more. Agreements of less than a year can be oral.

Different types of tenancy

There are different tenancy types in the private sector, differing according to when they were entered into. In the case of assured tenancies they will differ depending on what landlord and tenant agreed between themselves. The different types of tenancy are:

- Protected tenancy.
- Statutory tenancy.

- Assured tenancy.
- Short assured tenancy.

Protected tenancies

Before 1989, most private sector tenancies were likely to be protected tenancies. A protected tenancy is a contractual tenancy covered by the Rent Act (Scotland) 1984 and must satisfy the following requirements:

- The house must be let as a dwelling house (this can apply to a house or part of a house).
- The house must be a separate dwelling.
- The ratable value must be less than a specified sum.

Various categories of dwellings did not qualify as protected tenancies. A protected tenancy retains its status until the death of a tenant or his spouse, or any eligible successor, and therefore some protected tenancies are still in existence today.

Grounds for possession

As is the case in England and Wales, where there is no protected tenancy, the landlord may possess a property only by obtaining a court order. The landlord must serve a notice to quit, giving 28 days notice. A ground for possession must be shown, either discretionary or mandatory before possession can be given.

The grounds for possession are similar to those in England and Wales, with ten mandatory and ten discretionary grounds applying.

Fair rent system

A fair rent system, similar to England and Wales, exists in Scotland for protected tenants. There is a set procedure to be followed, with either the landlord or tenant, or jointly, making an application to the rent officer.

Once fixed, the rent is valid for three years. A fresh application can be made within three years if circumstances relating to the tenancy radically alter, such as a substantial refurbishment.

Statutory tenancies

A statutory tenancy is one which arises when a tenant remains in possession of a house after the contractual tenancy has been terminated (e.g. by a notice to quit) or a tenant has previously succeeded to the tenancy before 1990. A statutory tenant has similar rights to a protected tenant.

Assured tenants

Under the Housing (Scotland) Act 1988, the assured tenancy was introduced into Scotland coming into force after 2nd January 1989. This is very similar indeed to the assured tenancy introduced into England and Wales in 1989.

A Scottish assured tenancy has three elements:

- The tenancy must be of a house or flat or self contained dwelling. For an agreement to exist, there must be an agreement, rent payable, a termination date and possession, as there is in all leases in Scotland.
- The house must be let as a separate dwelling. A tenancy may be of a flat, part of a house, or even a single room, provided it is possible for the tenant to carry on all 'the major activities of residential life there, i.e. sleeping, cooking and feeding.
- The tenant must be an individual. A company cannot be given an assured tenancy.

The list of exclusions from assured tenancy status are the same as those in England and all the other provisions concerning rent, sub-letting succession, security of tenure and so on, apply.

The grounds for possession and the law governing termination of tenancies is a reflection of English Law.

Short-assured tenancies
The Housing Act (Scotland) also introduced 'short assured tenancies', a distinct form of assured tenancy for a fixed term of six months. Again, this is a reflection of the assured shorthold with the same provisions applying. The short assured tenant has little security of tenure. See appendix for an example of tenancy and notice (AT5) which must be served on the tenant prior to entering into the agreement stating that the agreement is a short assured tenancy. The following are the conditions for the creation of a short assured tenancy:

- The tenancy fulfills the requirements of a valid assured tenancy.
- The landlord, before the creation of the tenancy, has served on the tenant a formal notice (AT5) stating that the proposed tenancy is to be a short assured. tenancy and giving various information set out in regulations.
- The tenancy is for a fixed period of not less than six-months (there is no maximum period).

One main difference between assured shorthold tenancies and short assured is that, if neither landlord nor tenant take any action to renew the tenancy at the end of the fixed period (6 months) then the tenancy will automatically renew for the same minimum fixed period (or one year if the fixed period was more than one year). This is known as tacit relocation.

Recovery of possession
A short assured tenant has no defence to a properly based possession action. The sheriff must grant an order for possession if he is satisfied that all of the following apply:
- The tenancy has reached its termination date.
- No tacit relocation is in action (i.e. a valid notice to quit of at least 40 days has been served by the landlord.
- No further contractual tenancy is in existence.
- The landlord has given at least two months notice to the tenant that

he requires possession of the house. The notice can be served during the tenancy or after the termination date.

As with the English Assured shorthold, the landlord does not need to give any reason why he needs possession. In addition, because the short assured tenancy is a type of assured tenancy then recovery using the grounds for possession is the same as the assured tenancy. It can be seen that, apart from a number of minor differences, there are many similarities between the assured shorthold and the short assured tenancy.

Now read the main points from Chapter Nineteen.

Main points from Chapter Nineteen

- Private sector tenancies in Scotland are regulated by the Housing (Scotland) Act 1988.

- Agreements of 1 year or more must be in writing. Agreements for less than 1 year can be verbal.

- The most common form of private sector tenancy is the short assured tenancy.

- There are many similarities between the short assured tenancy and the assured shorthold tenancy.

Useful addresses and websites

The Buying Process

The Local Government Association
www.lganet.gov.uk
Confederation of Scottish Local Authorities
www.cosla.gov.uk
Greater London Authority
www.london.gov.uk
The Environment Agency
www.environment-agency.gov.uk
www.homecheckuk.com

House Prices

Halifax www.halifax.co.uk
Nationwide www.nationwide.co.uk
Land Registry www.landreg.gov.uk

Buying agents

Home Search Bureau www.homesearchbureau.co.uk

Property search sites

www.hometrack.co.uk
www.rightmove.co.uk
www.assertahome.co.uk
www.propertyfinder.co.uk
www.primelocation.com
www.findaproperty.com
www.thisislondon.co.uk

The buying and selling process

The Law Society www.lawsoc.org.uk
The Council of Mortgage Lenders www.cml.org.uk
HM Customs and Revenue www.inlandrevenue.co.uk

Scotland

Law Society of Scotland www.scotlaw.org.uk

Leasehold/freehold

Lease www.lease-advice.org
Association of Residential Managing Agents
www.arma.org.uk

Mortgage search sites/brokers

Money facts www.moneyfacts.co.uk
www.moneysupermarket.co.uk
www.moneynet.co.uk

New homes

NHBC www.nhbc.co.uk
National Home Owners Association www. nhoa.com

Renting and Letting

Association of Residential Letting Agencies (ARLA)
ARLA Administration
Maple House
53-55 Woodside Road
Amersham
Bucks
HP6 6AA

Tel: 01923 896555
Website: www.arla.co.uk
Email: info@arla.co.uk

Specialist rental property sites
www.letonthenet.com
www.lettingweb.com

Auctions
www.propwatch.com

Index

Allowable expenses, 9, 136
Area, 3, 13, 69
Areas of Outstanding Natural
    Beauty, 18
Assured shorthold tenancy, 106
Assured Shorthold tenancy, 8, 108
Assured tenancies, 106, 114
Assured tenancy, 145
Auction, 36, 37

Bankruptcy, 6, 75, 76
Brokers, 5, 42
Building Guarantees, 19
Building societies, 41
Buildings insurance, 33
Buying a listed building, 3, 18
Buying abroad, 89
Buying an old house, 3, 16
Buying Overseas, 7, 89
Buying with a friend, 4, 36

Capital allowance, 139
Capital gains tax, 9, 140, 143
Cashbacks, 48
Centralised lenders, 4, 41
Choosing your property, 3, 14
Coal mining search, 69
Commonhold, 15, 62
Commonhold and Leasehold Reform
    Act 2002, 15
Company lets, 7, 93, 94
Completing a sale, 4, 36
Completion, 6, 7, 74, 86
Conservation areas, 18
Contract for sale, 70
Conveyancing, 5, 30, 60, 77, 85, 157

Costs of moving, 34

Damages, 119
Death of a tenant, 9, 135
Death of Vendor, 76
Deposit, 4, 29, 98, 104, 129
Deposits, 7, 98
Disabled Facilities Assistance, 126
Disabled facilities grant, 3, 17
Disabled Facilities Grant, 125
Disabled tenants, 8, 121

Electrical Equipment (Safety)
    Regulations 1994, 125
Electrical Safety, 125
Endowment, 46, 47
Energy Performance Certificates
    (EPC's), 31
Equalities Act 2010, 3, 17
Estate Agents, 3, 5, 14, 25, 26, 29
Estates Gazette, 36
Exchange of contracts, 4, 36
Exchange of missives, 6, 82
Exchanging contracts, 6, 74

Fast track possession, 112

Financial Ombudsman Service, 49
Financial Services Act 1986, 71
Foreign currency mortgages, 48
Freehold property, 5, 60
French Property News, 89
Furnished holiday lettings, 9, 136,
    138, 141
Furniture, 102, 124

Gas Appliances(Safety) Regulations 1995, 124
Gas Cooking Appliances (safety) Regulations 1989, 124
Gas safety, 123, 124
Gas safety (Installation and use) Regulations 1998, 124
Georgian Group, 16
Grounds for possession, 8, 10, 110, 145

Halifax, 14, 27, 150
Heating Appliances(Fireguard) (safety) Regulations 1991, 124
Historic Scotland, 18
HMRC, 137, 139, 142, 143
Holiday lets, 7, 96, 97
House swapping, 4, 38
Houses in Multiple Occupation, 8, 121
Housing (Scotland) Act 1988, 144, 146, 149
Housing Act 2004, 121

Insurance, 4, 7, 103
Interest only mortgage, 48

Joint mortgages, 46
Joint sole agents, 26
Joint tenancies, 8, 115

Land Registration Acts of 1925, 64
Land Registry, 14, 31, 34, 64, 65, 150
Law of Property Act (Miscellaneous provisions) 1988, 71
Leasehold, 103, 151
Leasehold property, 5, 61
Leasehold Reform Act 1993, 3, 15

Legal ownership of property, 5, 60
Letting Agents, 7, 91
Local authority searches, 5, 68
Local Land Charges Act 1975, 67
Local land charges search, 5, 66, 67
Losses, 9, 139

Making an offer, 4, 6, 35, 82
Misdescription, 6, 72
Misrepresentation, 6, 73
Missives concluded, 6, 83
Mixed mortgages, 48
Mortgage arrangement fees, 33
Mortgage fees, 4, 32
Mortgage indemnity insurance, 32
Multiple agency, 26

National Energy Services Scheme, 19
Non-allowable expenses, 9, 137
Non-disclosure, 6, 73

Pension mortgages, 47
Planning permission, 3, 17
Plugs and Sockets etc. (Safety) Regulations 1994., 125
Possession, 9, 128, 144
Purchasing a flat, 3, 14

Raising rent, 8, 112
Removals, 4, 33
Removers, 79
Renovation grants, 3, 17
Rental agencies, 92
Rental guarantees, 7, 100
Repairs, 8, 103, 118
Repayment mortgages, 47
Reporting repairs, 8, 119
Right to Buy, 20

Royal Institute of British Architects, 17
Royal Institute of Chartered Surveyors, 14, 17, 36

Sale by tender, 4, 38
Sanitation, 9, 126
Scotland, 6, 10, 18, 81, 82, 83, 84, 85, 87, 134, 144, 145, 146, 147, 149, 151
Scottish law, 144
Secretary of State for Wales, 18
Security of tenure, 8, 109
Self-build, 3, 21
Service charges, 103
Services, 7, 19, 49, 50, 71, 102, 136
Shared housing, 8, 121, 127
Shared ownership property, 20
Short-assured tenancies, 10, 147
Short-lets, 7, 95
Social Housing, 20
Sole agency selling., 26
Spain, 89, 90
Stamp duty, 4, 30, 34

Structural surveys, 4, 31
Student lets, 7, 95

Tenancy Deposit Protection Scheme, 98
The 1985 Landlord and Tenant Act, 103
The National House Building Council, 19
The public sector, 7, 93, 101
The tenancy agreement, 103
Torts (Interference with Goods Act 1977, 134

USA, 89, 90

Valuing a property, 14
Victorian Society, 16
Viewing properties, 3, 15
Warrant for Possession of Land 131

Yuppification, 13

****

Buying, Selling and Renting Property

www.straightforwardco.co.uk

All titles, listed below, in the Straightforward Guides Series can be purchased online, using credit card or other forms of payment by going to www.straightfowardco.co.uk A discount of 25% per title is offered with online purchases.

Law
A Straightforward Guide to:
Consumer Rights
Bankruptcy Insolvency and the Law
Employment Law
Private Tenants Rights
Family law
Small Claims in the County Court
Contract law
Intellectual Property and the law
Divorce and the law
Leaseholders Rights
The Process of Conveyancing
Knowing Your Rights and Using the Courts
Producing Your own Will
Housing Rights
The Bailiff the law and You
Probate and The Law
Company law
What to Expect When You Go to Court
Guide to Competition Law
Give me Your Money-Guide to Effective Debt Collection
Caring for a Disabled Child
the Debt Collecting Merry Go Round
Business law
Public law

General titles
Letting Property for Profit
Buying, Selling and Renting property
Buying a Home in England and France
Bookkeeping and Accounts for Small Business
Creative Writing
Freelance Writing
Writing Your own Life Story
Writing performance Poetry
Writing Romantic Fiction
Speech Writing
Teaching Your Child to Read and write
Teaching Your Child to Swim
Raising a Child-The Early Years
Creating a Successful Commercial Website
The Straightforward Business Plan
The Straightforward C.V.
Successful Public Speaking
Handling Bereavement
Play the Game-A Compendium of Rules
Individual and Personal Finance
Understanding Mental Illness
The Two-Minute Message
Guide to Self Defence
Buying a Used Car
Tiling for Beginners
Developing an Online Business
Buying and selling on Auction Sites

Go to:

www.straightforwardco.co.uk